N

A First Book
in
Comprehension, Précis and Composition

L. G. Alexander

Longman

LONGMAN GROUP UK LIMITED
Longman House, Burnt Mill
Harlow, Essex CM20 2JE, England
and Associated Companies throughout the world.

*First published *1965*
*New impressions *1966 (twice); *1967 (twice);*
*1968 (twice); *1969 (twice); *1970 (twice);*
*1971; *1972 (twice); *1974 (twice); *1975;*
*1976; *1977; *1978; *1979 (4-times);*
*1980; *1981; *1982; *1984; *1985; *1986 (twice);*
*1987 (twice); *1988 (twice); *1989; *1990*
*1991; 1992; * 1994*

Produced through Longman Malaysia, VVP
ISBN 0-582-52305-2

Contents

Introduction

Level

The purpose of this book is to provide the immediately-post-elementary student with guidance in his first steps in comprehension, précis and composition. Where English is taught as part of a general curriculum, this book may be begun after two years' study. Students attending intensive courses, however, should be ready to begin after as little as six months' study.

There is sufficient material in this book for two or three years' work – depending on the amount of time allotted to it. Though not consciously written as part of a series, *A First Book in Comprehension, Précis and Composition* is closely related to its predecessors, *Sixty Steps to Précis* and *Essay and Letter Writing*. On completing this book, the student is advised to go on to *Sixty Steps to Précis* and, at the same time, to begin Chapter 3 of *Essay and Letter Writing*. He will thus be systematically prepared for the Cambridge University Lower and Proficiency Examinations in English.

General Aims

This book is based on the idea that at the earliest possible stages of learning, comprehension précis and composition amount to the same thing. The student needs practice in writing sentences and joining them together to form paragraphs. Though books on structural grammar may provide practice in writing sentences, the student often finds it immensely difficult to carry over the skills he has learnt from a grammar book to précis and composition writing. In the first three chapters the student will learn all he needs to know about simple, compound, and complex sentences. At the same time, he will be trained to write *continuous prose*. It is only in the last chapter that comprehension, précis and composition are broken up into separate compartments.

Method

The aim has been to teach précis and composition *through* comprehension. That is, the student is required to derive *specific* information from each passage and then to put it together again to form a paragraph of his own. The amount of help he is given to do this gradually diminishes so that in the last chapter he should be fully capable of writing a simple form of précis and composition unaided.

Grading

The material has been carefully graded, both from the point of view of structure and vocabulary.

Structure. A full analysis of the structures which the student will be expected to use is given in the Note to the Teacher which precedes Chapter 1. This will enable the teacher to tell at a glance whether his pupils are ready for this book.

Vocabulary. With a small number of exceptions the words used have been drawn from *A General Service List of English Words.* The *actual* vocabulary range in each chapter is as follows:

Chapter 1	600 words
Chapter 2	1000 words
Chapter 3	1400 words
Chapter 4	1800 words

The passages increase in length and complexity as the student progresses.

Chapter Introductions

Each chapter is preceded by detailed Introductions addressed to the teacher and the student. In the early chapters the instructions to the student have been sufficiently simplified to enable him to work on his own. Satisfactory results will be obtained *only* if the instructions given are scrupulously followed.

Chapter 1
The simple sentence

To the teacher

1   *AIMS*
(a) To enable the student to write simple sentences.
(b) To enable the student to put these sentences together to form a continuous paragraph.
(c) To help the student to grasp the basic word order in an English sentence: Subject/Verb/Object/Qualifying Phrases.

2   *HOW THE STUDENT SHOULD WORK*
The questions on the passages have been designed to elicit *simple* sentences from the student. These sentences should be written in a logical sequence as *continuous prose* so that the student's answers to the questions will form a single paragraph which, at the same time, will be a summary of the passage. Each exercise, therefore, will provide the student with simultaneous practice in comprehension, precis, and composition.

(a) *Question and Answer*
The student will be expected to derive *all* his information from the pieces. The questions do not always follow each passage closely, the aim being, where possible, to encourage the student to use his own words.

Teachers should insist on a *full* answer to each question. Short answers like, 'Yes, he did', 'No, he did not', etc., should not be given. To prevent the student from writing short answers, most questions beginning with 'Did' (or any other auxiliary verb) have been phrased as follows:
Did the man go into the house or not?
or: Did the man go into the house, or did he stay in the garden?

(b) *Word Order*
In order to help the student to grasp the basic Subject/Verb/Object/Qualifying Phrases pattern of an English sentence, the teacher should, at this stage, make every effort to discourage his pupils from separating a subject from its verb and a verb from its object. The only exception to this rule will be in the case of adverbs of frequency (always, ever, never, often, etc.). The teacher should

point out that time phrases ('in the morning', 'last week', 'yesterday', etc.) may be placed *before* the subject or *after* the object.

For example, the answer to a question might be:

Subject	Verb	Object	Qualifying Phrases
I	met	George	last week

Or: Qualifying Phrases		Subject	Verb	Object
Last week		I	met	George

The only exception to this rule will be where an adverb of frequency must be included in the answer in connection with the simple present tense:

Subject		Verb	Object
I	*often*	meet	George

At the outset, however, changing the position of a time phrase should be the only experiment with word order the student should allow himself. He should be told that the position of qualifying phrases in his responses will normally depend on the word order of the question.

3 VOCABULARY RANGE

At this stage, the student should have a *passive* vocabulary of about 800 words. The *actual* range is 600 words. The pieces are based on the most commonly used 600 words in the English language (with a small number of exceptions). The passages have been graded in order of increasing difficulty.

4 LENGTH OF EACH PASSAGE

About 80 words (single paragraphs).

5 LENGTH OF SUMMARIES

This will vary according to the passage. The exact number of words required for each summary has been pre-calculated and is about 45 words.

6 STRUCTURES

The passages contain simple and compound sentences, but very few complex sentences. The word order follows a simple pattern and the sentences are short and easy to understand. The active voice has been used throughout.

Here is a brief summary of the main structures the student will be expected to use (as distinct from those he will be required to recognize):

(a) *Articles*
Elementary uses of 'a' and 'the'.

(b) *Nouns*
Forming the plural with 's'. (Exceptions: money, advice).

(c) *Pronouns*
Personal and possessive. The use of apostrophe s. The use of 'one' in place of a noun. (e.g. 'the new one').

(d) *Adjectives*
Cardinal and ordinal numbers.
Position before a noun.
Regular comparison: er, est.
Irregular comparison: more . . . than.

(e) *Verbs*
Tenses: Continuous Present (Also as a future substitute).
Simple Present.
Simple Past (regular and irregular).
Past Continuous.
Present Perfect (Simple).
Simple Future (with 'shall', 'will', 'going to').

Auxiliary Verbs: will/would, can/could, have to/must/had to.
Verb+infinitive: begin to, decide to, learn how to, like to, want to (Exception: let+verb).

Phrasal Expressions: to be afraid of, to be in charge of, to call a number, to cry out, to feel angry, to go on a trip, to tell a lie/the truth.

Irregular Verbs: be, become, break, build, buy, catch, cost, drive, eat, feel, find, get, go, have, hear, lead, learn, leave, let, lie, meet, ring, run, say, see, sit, speak, spend, take, tell, and throw.

(f) *Adverbs*
Formation with 'ly' ('carefully', 'slowly' etc.).
Formation with 'ily' ('heavily').
Exception: 'late'.

(g) *Prepositions*
about, across, after, along, down, during, for, from, in, into, near, of, on, out, round, to, towards, through, up.

(h) *Miscellaneous Grammatical Points*
The use of 'ago'.
Anything/nothing, something/nothing, anyone/no one.
Of age/old (seventeen years of age/old).

4

Days of the week, months, seasons.
The date.
Direct and indirect object: to give someone something/to
                              give something to someone.
Ever/never. (Question and answer).
Impersonal subject: It is/was. There is/was.
Kind of/kinds of (+agreement of noun).
Much/many/a lot of/few.
Negatives with 'do' and 'did'.
Say/tell.
Telling the time.
This/that.
Too/very.

(i) *Phrases*
    This morning, in the evening, last Saturday, the other day, the next day, one night, in winter, next year, at first, at last, in the end, just then, a long time, a short time, each other, for lunch, for tea, a lot of trouble, by air.

To the student

There are twenty pieces in this chapter. You will answer questions on each piece. At the same time, you will learn how to write short, simple sentences. In each exercise you will put these sentences together and make a short paragraph.

Before you begin each piece, read these instructions *very* carefully:

How to Work
1   Read the piece carefully two or three times.
2   Write an answer to each question. Each answer must be a complete sentence.

3   Your answers must follow each other. All the sentences together will then make *a complete paragraph*.
4   Read through your work and correct your mistakes.
5   Count the number of words in your paragraph. Do not go over the word limit. At the end of your paragraph write the number of words that you have used.
6   Give your paragraph a title.

Now work through this example carefully and then try to do the exercises in the same way by yourself.

Example
Mr Johnson looked at his watch. It was half past seven. He got out of bed quickly. Then he washed and dressed. He was late as usual, so he did not have time for breakfast. He ran all the way to the station and he arrived there just in time for the train. Mr Johnson never eats anything in the morning. He always says to his friends at the office: 'It is nice to have breakfast in the morning, but it is nicer to lie in bed!'

QUESTIONS
Your answer must not be more than 45 words.

1   At what time did Mr Johnson get up?
2   Was he early, or was he late?
3   Did he have time for breakfast or not?
4   Where did he run?
5   Did he just catch the train, or did he miss the train?
6   Does Mr Johnson ever eat anything in the morning?
7   Does he prefer to have breakfast, or to lie in bed?

ANSWER
No Breakfast
Mr Johnson got up at half past seven. He was late. He did not have time for breakfast. He ran all the way to the station. He just caught the train. Mr Johnson never eats anything in the morning. He prefers to lie in bed.

45 Words.

1

I have a friend in England. His name is Ken Roberts. I know him very well, but I have never met him. We often write to each other. My letters are very short. It is still hard for me to write in English. I received a letter from Ken yesterday. It made me very happy. He is coming to my country for a holiday next year. We are going to see each other for the first time.

QUESTIONS
Your answer must not be more than 52 words.

1   Where does your friend, Ken Roberts, live?
2   Have you ever met him?
3   What do you both often do?
4   Are your letters short or long?
5   Is it hard for you to write in English, or is it easy?
6   What will Ken do next year?
7   Will you see each other for the first time or not?

2

I am learning how to drive a car. A week ago I had my first lesson. Yesterday my teacher took me out on a busy road. It was full of cars and people. I drove very slowly and carefully, but I felt afraid the whole time. At last the lesson finished and I went home. I felt very tired. I have learnt many things, but I have still got a lot to learn.

QUESTIONS

Your answer must not be more than 46 words.

1 What are you learning to do?
2 When did you have your first lesson?
3 Where did your teacher take you yesterday?
4 Did you drive quickly and carelessly or did you drive slowly and carefully?
5 How did you feel after the lesson?
6 Have you still got a lot to learn or not?

3

Our summer holidays last three months. During the last week of the holidays we get ready for school. We buy pencils, pens, paper, new books and copy books. On the first day of school we see all our old friends again and we tell them about the holidays. After that we go into class. It is so hard to keep quiet and pay attention to our teacher. He always says with a laugh, 'You forget more in three months than you learn in a year!'

QUESTIONS

Your answer must not be more than 55 words.

1 How long do our summer holidays last?
2 When do we prepare for school?
3 Whom do we see on the first day?
4 What do we tell them?
5 Where do we go then?
6 What does our teacher always say?

4

It is very hot in the summer and in the evenings nobody likes staying at home. People walk in the streets or sit in the open. We have a special summer cinema and my friends and I often go there. There are tall trees all round and it is very cool. Sometimes the films are not very good, but we do not mind. The stars shine in a clear sky and there is often a large bright moon. We can forget the film and enjoy a pleasant evening.

QUESTIONS
Your answer must not be more than 44 words.

1   Is it hot in the summer, or is it cold?
2   Do people like to go out in the evening, or do they like to stay at home? ·
3   Where do your friends and you often go?
4   Is it warm there, or is it cool?
5   Do you sometimes see bad films, or do you always see good films?
6   Do you mind about this or not?
7   Do you always enjoy a pleasant evening or not?

5

It is January 10th. Today Jane is seventeen years of age. She is wearing a pretty new dress. It is blue and white. Jane is having a party today and she is expecting all her friends to come. They are going to arrive in a short time. They are going to bring many beautiful presents with them. Jane's mother has prepared a lot of nice things to eat and drink. The young people are going to play games, sing, dance, and listen to music. They will have a wonderful time together.

QUESTIONS
Your answer must not be more than 51 words.

1   What is the date today?
2   Whose birthday is it?
3   How old is she?
4   Is Jane wearing a new dress, or is she wearing an old one?
5   Is she having a party or not?
6   When will her friends arrive?
7   What are the young people going to do at the party?

6

It is still winter, but on Sunday the weather was fine. We decided to go on a trip to the seaside. The sun was bright and warm, but we did not go into the water. It was too cold. Instead, we walked along the shore and looked at the ships. In the evening we returned home. Then a strong wind began to blow and it began to rain. So we sat round a warm fire. We did not mind about the weather at all.

QUESTIONS
Your answer must not be more than 44 words.

1   Is it still winter or summer?
2   Did we go to the seaside on Sunday or not?
3   Where did we walk?
4   What did we watch?
5   When did we reach home?
6   What happened then?
7   Where did we sit?

7

The young man heard a cry and turned round but he could not see anybody. At the same moment, a boy ran up to him and pointed towards the river. They both ran along the river bank and after a short time, they saw a girl in the water. The girl was holding on to a piece of wood, but the river was deep and it was carrying her away. The man acted quickly. He took off his coat at once, jumped into the water, and saved the girl's life.

QUESTIONS
Your answer must not be more than 43 words.

1   What did the young man hear?
2   Who ran up to him just then?
3   Where did the boy point?
4   Where did they both run?
5   What did they both see?
6   Did the man act quickly or did he act slowly?
7   Did he rescue the girl or not?

8

During the week-end I travelled by air for the first time in my life. I generally travel by train or bus. It is both cheaper and safer. But this was a short journey. At the beginning I did not feel very happy. This feeling did not last long. The trip was very exciting. I was soon high up in the sky among the clouds. The view of mountains, fields and rivers was interesting and unusual. I enjoyed my short and comfortable journey very much.

QUESTIONS

Your answer must not be more than 44 words.

1 When did you first travel by air?
2 Was it a short journey or was it a long one?
3 How did you feel at first?
4 Did this feeling soon pass or not?
5 What was the trip like?
6 Was the view of mountains, fields and rivers interesting or not?
7 Was the short journey comfortable, or was it uncomfortable?

9

Mr and Mrs Simms go to the market on Saturday mornings. Mr Simms never enjoys these visits. Mrs Simms goes shopping and he sits on a box and waits for her. This morning there was more noise than usual and everyone was in a hurry. Mrs Simms bought some meat, fish, fruit and vegetables. An hour passed and then a man came up to Mr Simms. 'Excuse me,' he said, 'is your name Simms? Your wife has finished shopping now, but her bags are very heavy. She wants you to carry them home for her.'

QUESTIONS

Your answer must not be more than 45 words.

1 Where do Mr and Mrs Simms go every Saturday morning?
2 Does Mr Simms enjoy it or not?
3 Did his wife buy many different things this morning, or did she buy only a few things?
4 How long did her husband wait?
5 What did Mrs Simms want her husband to do in the end?

10

Last week I went out to lunch with my friend George. George is very fat. He likes good food – and a lot of it. We sat at a table in a restaurant. The waiter brought a tray full of things. After a big meal we ate some cheese and drank some coffee. 'We really must go now George,' I said. 'We have been here for nearly three hours. It's ten to four.'
'What do you mean?' asked George in surprise. 'We can't leave now. It's time for tea!'

QUESTIONS
Your answer must not be more than 47 words.

1 Did George and I go to a restaurant for lunch or for dinner?
2 Is George fat or is he thin?
3 Does he like a lot of good food or not?
4 Did we eat a big meal, or did we eat a small one?
5 How long did we stay in the restaurant?
6 What time was it?
7 Did George want to leave, or did he want to stay?
8 Was it time for tea, or was it time for dinner?

11

I worked as a postman for a short time. But I am afraid of dogs and I had a lot of trouble. One day, I tried to deliver a post-card to a big house. I got off my bicycle and at once a large dog ran towards the gate. It made a lot of noise and in the end I dropped the card in the garden. The dog picked it up immediately and carried it into the house. The dog was a better postman than I was!

QUESTIONS

Your answer must not be more than 58 words.

1 Did I work as a postman for a long time or for a short time?
2 Did I find the work easy or did I find it difficult?
3 Do I like dogs, or am I afraid of them?
4 Where did I have to deliver a post-card one day?
5 Would the dog at the house let me go through the gate or not?
6 Where did I throw the card?
7 Where did the dog take it?

12

It rained heavily last winter and the little stream near our house became a big river. It burst its banks and the fields all round were soon full of water. Luckily, the water did not reach any of the houses in our village. But the river carried away our beautiful wooden bridge. The bridge was more than a hundred years old and we were sorry to lose it. We are building a new one now, but it will never be the same.

QUESTIONS

Your answer must not be more than 48 words.

1 When did the little stream near our house become a big river?
2 What happened to the fields all round?
3 Did the water reach any of the houses in our village or not?
4 What happened to our old wooden bridge?
5 What are we doing now?

13

'Did you buy anything new in Europe?' asked the Customs officer.
'Just a few small articles,' answered the lady. 'I didn't buy anything valuable.'
'May I open your case please?' asked the officer.
'Of course,' said the lady, 'but it's only full of dirty clothes.'
'That doesn't matter,' replied the officer. 'I'm used to that.'
At that moment, the lady's daughter, a little girl of six, cried out, 'Oh, you must not open that case. My mother has hidden her new gold watch in there. It's in her brown hand-bag!'

QUESTIONS
Your answer must not be more than 45 words.

1   Did the lady tell the Customs officer a lie or did she tell him the truth?
2   Did she say, 'I didn't buy anything valuable', or did she say 'I bought something valuable.'?
3   What did the officer want to open?
4   What did the lady's daughter do just then?
5   Did the child tell the officer the truth or not?
6   What was there in the suit-case?

14

The children next door often play football in the garden and sometimes break my windows. Last Saturday afternoon I stayed at home and read a book. After a while, I closed my eyes and went to sleep. A sound at the door made me get up quickly. Soon a little boy appeared.
'Not one of my windows again?' I asked.
'Oh, no!' answered the boy. 'Your window was open this time and our ball is in your bed-room. May we get it please?'

QUESTIONS

Your answer must not be more than 50 words.

1   Where do the children next door often play football?
2   What do they sometimes break?
3   Where did I spend the afternoon last Saturday?
4   Who came to the door?
5   What did he want to do?
6   Where was it?
7   Did he break my window or not?
8   Was it open, or was it shut?

15

Mrs Mills often spends too much money on clothes. She does not need new clothes, but she loves buying them. Yesterday she saw a beautiful coat in a shop window. She went in and put it on. It was just the right size, but it was very dear. Mrs Mills did not have enough money, but she took the coat home and showed it to her husband. He liked it very much, but he did not like the price. His wife gave him a bill for £80!

QUESTIONS

Your answer must not be more than 47 words.

1   Does Mrs Mills often waste money on clothes or not?
2   What did she see in a shop window yesterday?
3   Was it too small, too large, or just the right size?
4   Did Mrs Mills leave the coat in the shop, or did she take it home?
5   Whom did she want to pay for it?
6   Did he like the price?
7   How much did the coat cost?

16

There was a great deal of trouble in the city the other day. A horse got out of a field and came into town on its own. It walked across the Public Gardens and through a busy street. Then it sat down in the middle of the main road opposite a church. All the traffic stopped. Quite a few people tried to lead it away, but no one could move it. Just then, a farmer appeared. He called to it. It got up and he led it away.

QUESTIONS
Your answer must not be more than 47 words.

1   What caused a lot of trouble in the city the other day?
2   Where did it walk?
'3   Where did it sit?
4   Could anyone move it?
5   Who led it away in the end?

17

The telephone rang and I picked up the receiver.
'Hullo,' I said.
'Hullo,' said a voice. 'Bill here. Is Betty there?'
'I'm sorry,' I said, 'you've got the wrong number.'
A few seconds later, the telephone rang again. Just as I expected, it was Bill. 'You've made a mistake again,' I explained.
Then the phone rang a third time. This made me angry. I spoke in a high voice, 'Hullo, Bill. Betty here.'
For a moment there was complete silence. Then someone said, 'What's the *matter* with you Tom?'
It was my mother!

QUESTIONS
Your answer must not be more than 44 words.

1 How many times did a strange man telephone you?
2 What was his name?
3 Whom did he want to speak to?
4 Did he call the right number, or did he call the wrong number?
5 Did the phone ring a third time?
6 Did you feel angry, or did you feel pleased?
7 What did you say then?
8 Was it Bill or not?
9 Who was it?

18

Mr Dawson is the head of a large company. The other day, he was talking to his son.

'Well, Peter,' he said, 'you finished school five months ago. You really must think about the future. There are fine opportunities in the business for a clever young man like you. You will soon get experience. Who knows, in twenty years' time you may even have a position like mine. Of course, a little hard work will be necessary.'

'Yes, father,' replied Peter, 'but I don't want to work hard. I want to be an actor!'

QUESTIONS
Your answer must not be more than 51 words.

1 What is Mr Dawson in charge of?
2 The other day, was he giving his son some advice or not?
3 When did Peter leave school?
4 Did his father want him to enter the business or not?
5 What would Peter have to do?
6 Did he like the idea?
7 What did he want to become?

19

It was very dark. Two men were advancing slowly across the plain. Snow was lying on the ground and a cold wind was blowing. They noticed a light behind some trees and soon arrived at a house. A poor old man immediately invited them into a clean room. He seemed a strange fellow, but he spoke kindly and offered them milk and fresh fruit. The men remained there until morning. Then the man led them to the nearest village, but he would not accept any money for his help.

QUESTIONS
Your answer must not be more than 50 words.

1   Where were two men walking one cold, dark night?
2   Where did they arrive at last?
3   Who lived there?
4   Did he ask them in, or did he tell them to go away?
5   Did he give them a simple meal, or did he give them nothing at all?
6   Did the men stay there all night or did they leave immediately?
7   Where did the man take them next day?

20

After the war our church was in a very bad condition. So we decided to build a modern one at the top of a hill just outside the town. We used many different kinds of materials. We built the walls of stone and glass; the heavy doors of wood and metal. From the top of the church there is a wonderful view. You can see the entire town and countryside for miles around. People from all parts of the country visit the church every day. It is such an interesting building.

QUESTIONS

Your answer must not be more than 42 words.

1   When did we build a new church?
2   Did we build it at the top of a hill or did we build it at the bottom of a hill?
3   Did we use one kind of material or many different materials?
4   Is there a good view or a poor view of the town and countryside from the top?
5   Do few people visit the church every day, or do many people visit it?

Chapter 2
The compound sentence

To the teacher

1 *AIMS*
(a) To enable the student to write compound sentences.
(b) To enable the student to put these sentences together to form a continuous paragraph.
(c) To help the student to gain experience in handling conjunctions and connecting phrases.
(d) To provide revision practice in writing simple sentences (learned in the previous Chapter).

2 *HOW THE STUDENT SHOULD WORK*
The questions on the passages have been designed to elicit compound sentences from the student. As in the previous Chapter, these sentences should be written in a logical sequence as *continuous prose*. The student's answers to the questions should form a single paragraph.

(a) *Question and Answer*
The questions in this section differ in one important respect from those given in Chapter 1. In order to be able to write a compound sentence of his own, the student will have to answer two or sometimes three questions *in a single sentence*. The conjunctions the student should use are given in brackets at the end of each series of questions.

Here, for example, is a series of questions of this sort:
Whom did I ring up after breakfast? Did anyone answer? When did I telephone again? *(but) (so)*

The answer to these questions should be written in *one* sentence, using the conjunctions given in brackets:

After breakfast I rang up my friend Tim, but no one answered so I telephoned again at noon.

(b) *Word Order*
The basic S/V/O pattern should again be closely followed. In this chapter, however, the Subject will not always be a single word, but will frequently take the form of a phrase. For example:

Subject	Verb	Object	Qualifying Phrases
A man in a black coat	bought	a ticket	at the station

3 VOCABULARY RANGE

The student's *passive* vocabulary should be about 1200 words. The *actual* range (taking into account the words used in the previous Chapter) is about 1000 words. The passages have been graded in order of increasing difficulty.

4 LENGTH OF EACH PASSAGE

150–160 words (single paragraphs).

5 LENGTH OF SUMMARIES

70–80 words. The word limit should be strictly observed.

6 STRUCTURES

Though the active voice has again been employed throughout, the passages will now be found to contain *complex* sentences, in addition to simple and compound. The student will also be expected to use the past perfect (simple) tense. He should, furthermore, be completely familiar with the rules governing the sequence of tenses.

The *conjunctions* the student will be expected to use are as follows: and, and now, and so, and then, both . . . and, but, neither . . . nor, not only . . . but also, not only . . . but . . . as well, now, so, then, therefore.

Connecting words and phrases: personal pronouns, next day, just then, suddenly, at that moment, at this point, from there, last week, meanwhile, one night/day, in the end, there, this, some days later, immediately, soon, beyond, after, this time, in this way.

To the student

There are twenty pieces in this chapter and you will again answer questions on each piece. Now you will learn how to join simple sentences together with words like 'and', 'but', 'so', 'then' etc. We call 'joining words' of this sort, 'conjunctions'. Conjunctions help us to join different ideas together to make *compound* sentences.

Before you begin each piece, read these instructions *very* carefully:

How to Work
1   Read the passage carefully two or three times.
2   Write a full answer to each question. When you find two or three questions together, join up your answers with the conjunctions given in brackets. Each answer you write must be *a complete sentence.*
3   Your answers to the questions must follow each other. All the sentences together will then make *a complete paragraph.*
4   Read through your work and correct your mistakes.
5   Count the number of words in your paragraph. Do not go over the word limit. At the end of your paragraph write the number of words that you have used.
6   Give your paragraph a title.

Now work through this example carefully and then try to do the exercises in the same way by yourself.

Example
Nobody likes staying at home on a public holiday—especially if the weather is fine. Last August we decided to spend the day in the country. The only difficulty was that millions of other people had exactly the same idea.
5   We moved out of the city slowly behind a long line of cars, but at last we came to a quiet country road and, after some time, stopped at a lonely farm. We had

brought plenty of food with us and we got it out of the
car. Now everything was ready so we sat down near a
10 path at the foot of a hill. It was very peaceful in the cool
grass—until we heard bells ringing at the top of the hill.
What we saw made us pick up our things and run back
to the car as quickly as possible. There were about two
hundred sheep coming towards us down the path!

QUESTIONS
Your answer must not be more than 74 words.

1 Where did we decide to drive last August?
2 Were there a lot of cars on the road, or were there only a
few? Did it take us a long time to find a quiet place or
not? *(so)*
3 What did we get out of the car? Where did we sit? *(and)*
4 What did we hear soon afterwards? Where did we have
to run? *(and)*
5 What were coming down the path?

ANSWER
A Day in the Country
Last August we decided to drive into the country. There
were a lot of cars on the road *so* it took us a long time to
find a quiet place. We got our food out of the car *and* sat
down near a path at the foot of a hill. Soon afterwards, we
heard bells ringing *and* we had to run back to the car. About
two hundred sheep were coming down the path!

74 Words.

21

A guide warned us that we would have to climb 937 steps to reach the top of the ancient tower. At first we started counting the steps ourselves, but we soon lost patience. We occasionally passed small windows cut into the wall.
5   As these gave little light, we felt as if we were going round and round a dark tunnel. It was good to get out into the fresh air at last. From the top there was an excellent view of the grounds of the castle and of the surrounding countryside. In the distance, we could just see the remains
10 of an ancient wall; beyond this, we saw a park in which deer were wandering freely. Immediately below us, there was a big ditch with a bridge across it. The bridge was full of people – not enemy soldiers, but peaceful tourists like ourselves who had come to visit the castle and its
15 famous tower.

QUESTIONS

Your answer must not be more than 69 words.

1   Was it a long climb to the top of the ancient tower or not?
    Was the view of the castle grounds and the countryside
    very good from there, or was it very bad? *(but)*
2   Could we see a park beyond an old wall, or could we see
    a garden?
3   What kinds of animals were there?
4   What was just below us?
5   Was the bridge full of tourists, or was it full of soldiers?
6   What did they want to see?

22

After returning to the surface, the diver told the captain that he had at last found a metal safe in the sunken ship, but he said that it would be impossible to cut it open under the water. The captain decided that the best thing
5 to do would be to blow the safe up. The diver went down again with a number of explosives which he fitted to the doors of the safe and then he came up immediately. After a few minutes, the explosives were set off electrically, sending up a shower of water. When the water settled
10 again, the diver descended for a third time to examine the contents of the safe. The explosion had torn away the door. In the lamp light he caught sight of shining metal. Closer examination showed that there were neat piles of gold bars inside the safe. Very excited now, the diver
15 took one of the bars and returned once more to the waiting ship above.

QUESTIONS
Your answer must not be more than 72 words.

1 What did the diver find in the wreck? Could he open it or not? *(but)*
2 Did he go down again or not? What did he take with him? *(and)*
3 Did he return to the ship above once more, or did he stay under the sea? Where did he go after the underwater explosion? *(and then)*
4 What did he see inside the safe this time?
5 What did he take? Did he return to the surface at once, or did he stay in the ship-wreck? *(and)*

23

The train I was travelling on was already half an hour
late. I had arranged to arrive in Vienna at 7.15 in time to
catch the 7.25 train to Paris—but there was no hope of
that now. I explained the situation to the ticket-collector
5 who advised me to get off two stops before Vienna
Central Station and take a taxi. When the time came, he
even helped me with my luggage. He wished me good
luck as I jumped off, and a few minutes later I was
racing towards the centre of the city in a taxi. It was
10 almost 7.25 when we stopped outside the station. I paid
the driver quickly, seized my bags and hurried inside.
'Paris train?' was all I had time to say to the first official
I saw. You can imagine my disappointment when he
pointed to a train that was just moving out of the station
15 at great speed!

QUESTIONS
Your answer must not be more than 72 words.

1   Was my train to Vienna going to arrive on time or not?
    What did I want to do in Vienna? *(and)*
2   To whom did I turn for help?
3   What did he tell me to do?
4   Did I take his advice or not? Did I arrive at the station
    late, or was I just in time? *(and so)*
5   Did I enter the station quickly, or did I go in slowly?
    Was the train standing in the station, or was it just
    leaving? Did I catch it, or did I miss it? *(but) (and)*

24

My friend Jones is not a very practical person. Driving
along a main road one dark night he suddenly had a flat
tyre. Even worse, he discovered that he did not have a
spare wheel in the back of his car! Jones waved to
5 passing cars and lorries, but not one of them stopped.
Half an hour passed and he was almost in despair. At
last he waved to a car just like his own. To his surprise,
the car actually stopped and a well-dressed young
woman got out. Jones was terribly disappointed. How
10 could a person like this possibly help him? The lady,
however, offered him her own spare wheel, but Jones had
to explain that he had never changed a wheel in his life!
She set to work at once and fitted the wheel in a few
minutes while Jones looked on in admiration.

QUESTIONS
Your answer must not be more than 69 words.

1   What sort of person is Jones?
2   Did he have a flat tyre one dark night or not? Did he
    have a spare wheel with him or not? *(not only . . . but)*
3   For how long did he wave to passing cars? Who stopped
    in the end? *(and)*
4   What did she offer him? Was he able to fit it or not?
    What did she do? *(but) (so)*
5   What did Jones do meanwhile?

25

Last year we visited a large modern factory where they make window glass. We first saw workmen mixing sand and other materials together in the right amounts. Then they added some broken glass to the mixture as this helps
5 it to melt. They then fed the mixture into a big hot oven. At the far end of the oven, a stream of liquid glass came out. Here some men lowered a metal frame into the liquid. As the frame came up, it pulled away a hot sheet of glass. Special rollers took hold of the sheet at either
10 side and carried it upwards. Our guide told us that at this stage it was necessary for the glass to cool slowly as this would make it very strong. At a height of 30 feet, the sheet of glass became cool and another machine cut it into big pieces which workmen stored away together.
15 The glass was now ready for use.

QUESTIONS

Your answer must not be more than 75 words.

1   What sort of factory did we visit last year?
2   Where did workmen put the mixture of sand and other materials?
3   What came out at one end of the oven? What did a metal frame draw up? *(and)*
4   At what height did the glass become cool? Did workmen cut it into small pieces, or did a machine cut it into big pieces? *(and)*
5   Was the glass now ready for use or not? What did workmen do with it? *(and)*

26

It was the ambition of an eleven year old boy in Kansas
City to be an engine-driver. Born without arms, he had
been to special schools where he learned to use his feet
as 'hands'. He spent all his spare time watching trains
5 and one day his dreams came true. Seeing a deserted
engine, the boy climbed in. He had no difficulty in starting it up with his feet. Soon he was travelling along at
forty miles an hour. Signalmen could not see the young
driver, so they set out to stop the train. Meanwhile the
10 boy reached Missouri, stopped the engine himself, and
then made it go backwards. When he was near home, a
railway-man caught up with the engine and stopped it.
At first he was very angry, but he smiled when the boy
said simply, 'I like trains.'
15 'Well, I'm glad you don't like planes!' answered the
railway-man.

QUESTIONS
Your answer must not be more than 80 words.

1 What had an eleven year old boy without arms learned
at a school in Kansas City?
2 What was his ambition?
3 What did he see one day? Did he start it up or not?
Did he get as far as Missouri or not? *(and . . . not only
. . . . but)*
4 Did he get out then, or did he make the train go backwards? Who stopped it? *(but)*
5 What did the boy say to him?
6 Did the railway-man smile or not? What did he answer?
(then)

27

I always have a difficult time choosing original birthday
presents. My imagination never seems to get beyond ties,
handkerchiefs, or pairs of socks. But, strangely enough,
it did not take me long to decide on Tom's birthday
5 present. For the first time in my life I had a good idea – I
would buy him a bottle of champagne. Before the party
began, Tom suggested that I should open the bottle. I
put it between my knees and began to pull, but it remained
firmly corked. Soon a crowd gathered round to watch the
10 fight between me and the bottle. I could hear all sorts of
'helpful' suggestions from the guests like 'Break the top
off!', 'Use your teeth!' etc., but I was losing the battle.
We were struggling on the floor together, when all of a
sudden there was a loud 'pop!' and the cork shot up into
15 the air, while the angry bottle showered everybody with
champagne!

QUESTIONS
Your answer must not be more than 67 words.

1 Is it always easy for me to choose original birthday
   presents, or do I find it difficult? Did I buy an unusual
   one for my friend Tom or not? *(but)*
2 What was it?
3 Who asked me to open it before the party?
4 Did the guests look on or not? Did they make 'helpful'
   suggestions or not? Could I open the bottle easily or not?
   (and) *(but)*
5 What did I hear after a long struggle? What did the
   bottle do? *(and)*

28

When the woman opened the door she guessed at once that the man was a prisoner of war. There was mud on his face and on his torn clothes. He asked for food and shelter. He told the woman that a 'friend' had given him
5 her address. She immediately asked what the name of the friend was, but he replied that he had forgotten. This made the woman suspicious. She knew that the enemy was making every effort to prevent the local people from helping prisoners. Deciding not to take the risk, she told
10 the man she could not help him. For days she wondered whether she had acted rightly–until she heard that enemy soldiers had arrested a neighbour for helping a 'prisoner of war'. The arrest put the villagers on their guard, for they realized that the enemy had sent out specially
15 trained soldiers who pretended to be prisoners who had escaped.

QUESTIONS
Your answer must not be more than 75 words.

1 What did the man at the door appear to be?
2 Who did he say had given him the woman's address? Could he remember his name or not? *(but)*
3 Did this information make the woman suspicious or not? Did she let the man in or did she refuse to let him in? *(so)*
4 What did enemy soldiers do some days later?
5 What had he (the neighbour) done?
6 What was this 'prisoner' really? What effect did the arrest have on the villagers? *(and)*

29

I always settle down comfortably in the barber's shop and
listen patiently to my barber. He explains the present
political situation, women's fashions, or tells me jokes
which I have heard at least five times already. In twenty
5 minutes I get a remarkable amount of information, as
well as a hair-cut. But last week our conversation was
very short indeed. We heard loud cries of 'Fire!' coming
from upstairs. Customers and barbers rushed out of the
shop immediately. We were certainly a funny sight to
10 passers-by! I had a white sheet round my neck and my
hair was half cut. My barber was close behind me with
a comb and a pair of scissors in his hands. The man who
had sat next to me was not so lucky. There was soap on
one side of his face and his barber ran after him holding
15 a shaving-brush in one hand and a razor in the other!

QUESTIONS

Your answer must not be more than 81 words.

1   Do I enjoy my visits to the barber or not?
2   Do I learn many things from him or not? Do I have a
     hair-cut or do I have a shave? *(not only . . . but also)*
3   Did our talk last a long time last week, or did it last a
     short time?
4   What did we hear? Did we stay in the shop or did we
     run outside? *(and)*
5   How did we look to passers-by?
6   What did I have round my neck? What did another man
     have on his face? *(and)*
7   What was my barber holding?
8   What was the other one holding?

30

When the balloon rose to 3000 feet, the pilot took off his ear-pads. He had been wearing them ever since the balloon had left the ground so as not to hear the noise of the hot-air fans. All at once, he heard a small, frightened
5 voice below him calling, 'Sir, would you please help me?' Looking down, the pilot saw a boy about twelve years old holding on to a rope. He immediately shouted back, 'Hold on . . . don't look at the ground . . . look at me.' The balloon descended slowly and the boy was soon
10 safe on the ground again. As the pilot learned later, the boy had been eager to help before the balloon took off. Together with others, he had held on to the heavy ropes. The pilot had signalled 'Let go!' Everybody did so— except the boy who had tied the rope to his wrist and he
15 was soon sailing through the air.

QUESTIONS
Your answer must not be more than 74 words.

1 What did the pilot of the balloon take off at 3000 feet? What did he hear? *(and then)*
2 Who was holding on to a rope below the balloon? Did the pilot immediately return to earth or not? *(so)*
3 When had the boy taken hold of the rope?
4 What signal had the pilot given? Could the boy obey the signal or not? *(but)*
5 What had he tied to his wrist?

31

As soon as Mr and Mrs Groves moved into their charming old house in the country, they decided to scrape away all the faded green wall-paper from the walls. They began with the living-room. Mr Groves got a ladder
5 from the garden, while his wife brought in a bucket of water. Then they wetted the paper well until it became soft. In this way, they were able to scrape it off easily. After three hours' hard work, when they were both beginning to feel rather tired, Mr Groves pulled away a
10 long strip of paper over the fireplace. He called out excitedly to his wife. The former owner had written these words on the wall: 'We hope you enjoy making this room look beautiful as much as we did. Don't work too hard. Make yourselves a cup of tea!' 'What a good idea!'
15 said Mrs Groves, and she hurried into the kitchen.

QUESTIONS
Your answer must not be more than 74 words.

1   Did Mr and Mrs Groves move into a new house, or did they move into an old one?
2   What was on the walls? What did they decide to do? *(and)*
3   What did they do to the paper in the living-room? Did it come off easily or not? *(so)*
4   How long did they work? How did they feel? *(and)*
5   Did Mr Groves call to his wife just then or not?
6   Where had the former owner written the words 'Make yourselves a cup of tea'?
7   Did Mrs Groves act on his advice or not?

32

Science has told us so much about the moon that it is
fairly easy to imagine what it would be like to go there.
It is certainly not a friendly place. As there is no air or
water, there can be no life of any kind. There is no variety
5 of scenery either. For mile after mile there are only flat
plains of dust with mountains around them. Above, the
sun and stars shine in a black sky. If you step out of the
mountain shadows, it will mean moving from severe
cold into great heat. These extreme temperatures con-
10 tinually break rocks away from the surface of the
mountains. The moon is also a very silent world, for
sound waves can only travel through air. But beyond the
broken horizon, you see a friendly sight. Our earth is
shining more brightly than the stars. From this distance,
15 it looks like an immense ball, coloured blue and green
and brown.

QUESTIONS
Your answer must not be more than 78 words.

1   Is the moon a friendly place, or is it an unfriendly place?
2   Is there any air or water there? Is there any life or not?
     Is there any variety of scenery or not? *(so . . . neither
     . . . nor)*
3   Do the sun and stars shine in a black sky, or do they
     shine in a blue sky? What effect do the extremes of
     temperature have on the rocks? *(and)*
4   Can sound waves travel on the moon or not? What is the
     effect of this? *(so)*
5   How does the earth appear from there?

33

In the darkness I leant over the railings and watched the ship cutting a path through the waves. It was pleasant to be on board on such a fine night. But the captain had told me that the ship would arrive at five o'clock in the
5 morning. I therefore decided to return to my cabin because I wanted to get up early to take some photographs as the boat entered the harbour. It was very hot below and, in spite of my good intentions, I lay awake for hours listening to the ship's engines. At last I went to
10 sleep, but the noise made by heavy chains and the sound of the ship's whistle soon woke me up. I dressed hurriedly, seized my camera, and rushed outside. Then I had an unpleasant surprise. The fine view I expected to see had disappeared. The ship had entered the harbour
15 long before!

QUESTIONS
Your answer must not be more than 82 words.

1　What time did they expect the ship to arrive at the harbour? Did the writer go to bed early or late? *(so)*
2　What did he want to do next day?
3　Was it hot in his cabin, or was it cold? Did it take him a long time to get to sleep or not? *(and)*
4　Did the ship's whistle suddenly wake him up or not?
5　Did he get dressed quickly, or did he get dressed slowly? Did he hurry outside or not? Was it too early, or was it too late? *(and) (but)*
6　When had the ship come into the harbour?

34

A motorist saw two men walking along a lonely country road. They were carrying heavy bags, so he at once informed the police. That morning the police had broadcast a message on the radio asking for information
5 which might lead to the arrest of two thieves who had stopped a train and stolen mail-bags containing a lot of money. The police soon arrived on the scene. They questioned both men but neither of them could speak English. The men tried hard to resist arrest and kept
10 shouting loudly at the police all the way to the station. When they arrived there, both men refused to say anything and simply pointed at their bags. The police opened them at once and then realized that they had made a terrible mistake. The men were French onion-sellers and
15 their bags were full of onions! Apologizing for their mistake, the police set the men free immediately.

QUESTIONS
Your answer must not be more than 69 words.

1 Whom did the police want to catch? Did they ask for help or not? *(and)*
2 Whom was a motorist suspicious of?
3 What were they carrying? What did he do? *(so)*
4 Did the police find the men or not? Could they understand their language or not? Where did they take them? *(but) (so)*
5 What did they open there?
6 What were the bags full of?
7 What were the men? Did the police put them in prison, or did they let them go? *(so)*

35

Henry Ford was the first person to build cars which were cheap, strong, and fast. He was able to sell millions of models because he 'mass-produced' them; that is, he made a great many cars of exactly the same type. Ford's
5 father hoped that his son would become a farmer, but the young man did not like the idea and he went to Detroit where he worked as a mechanic. By the age of 29, in 1892, he had built his first car. However, the first 'mass-produced' car in the world, the famous 'Model T',
10 did not appear until 1908 – five years after Ford had started his great Motor Company. This car proved to be so popular that it remained unchanged for twenty years. Since Ford's time, mass-production methods have become common in industry and have reduced the price
15 of many articles which would otherwise be very expensive.

QUESTIONS
Your answer must not be more than 71 words.

1 Did Henry Ford mass-produce cars, or did he make them by hand? Did he sell a great many models, or did he sell only a few? *(so)*

2 What did Ford's father want his son to be? Where did the young man go? What did he do there? *(but) (and)*

3 Did he start a Motor Company or not? When did he build the world's first mass-produced car? *(and)*

4 What did he call it?

5 Was it very popular or not? For how long did it remain unchanged? *(and)*

6 Have mass-production methods made industrial goods cheap or expensive since Ford's time?

36

As neither she nor her husband smoked, Mrs Trench was
surprised to see cigarette ash on her doorstep as she
entered the house. When she opened the living-room
door, an extraordinary sight met her eyes. A strange man
5 had taken advantage of her absence and was fast asleep
in an armchair! Taking care not to disturb him, Mrs
Trench left the house immediately. She called a taxi and
went straight to the police station. When she got there,
she hastily explained what had happened and added
10 that the man must have got into the house through an
open window. Mrs Trench returned home in a police car
together with two policemen. But it was now too late:
the man had disappeared. Hurrying upstairs, she went to
her dressing-table. She smiled with relief when she saw
15 that the only thing the man had taken was an imitation
diamond necklace which was almost worthless!

QUESTIONS
Your answer must not be more than 71 words.

1 What did Mrs Trench see on her front doorstep? Did
   this surprise her or not? *(and)*
2 Where did she go then? Did she get a shock, or was she
   pleased? *(and)*
3 Who was sleeping in an armchair?
4 Where did Mrs Trench immediately go? With whom did
   she return? Was the man still there, or had he left?
   (and) (but)
5 Did she hurry upstairs, or did she talk to the policemen?
6 What had the man stolen from her dressing-table?
7 Was it valuable or not? Did she feel relieved, or did she
   feel angry? *(so)*

37

'Now for the run home . . . I wonder if we can do it,'
wrote Captain Scott at the South Pole. The 'run home'
was a journey of 900 miles on which five men of great
courage lost their lives. Fierce winds blew against them
5 across a desert of snow and ice and they could walk only
a few miles each day. A month later Evans died after a
serious accident. Soon, another member of the party,
Captain Oates, could go no further. One morning he
said, 'I am just going outside and may be some time.'
10 He disappeared into the snow and never returned. Three
men now struggled on until they were only eleven miles
from their base-camp where there was plenty of food.
But a terrible snow-storm began and they had to remain
in their tent for days. A search party found their bodies a
15 year later. All three had died in their sleep.

QUESTIONS

Your answer must not be more than 70 words.

1   How many miles was the return journey from the South
    Pole? Was the weather good or bad? Could Captain
    Scott and his four companions cover a great many miles
    each day or only a few? *(but) (so)*
2   Which two men died on the way? *(Both . . . and)*
3   What did the other men now try to reach?
4   How far away was it? What kept them in their tent?
    What happened to the three men? *(but) (and)*

38

A heavy load of wine barrels made it difficult for the lorry to climb the hill. Near the top, the driver had to stop suddenly to avoid hitting a log which was lying in the middle of the road. Immediately there was a loud
5 crash from behind. The driver looked out of the window and noticed that one of the barrels had slid off the back. As there was no hope of getting it back now, the man drove away. Meanwhile, the barrel was travelling at full speed down the hill. It narrowly missed a lamp post and
10 then it changed direction and struck a tree with great force. The noise woke up an old beggar who was sleeping by the roadside. He jumped up with a shock and it nearly broke his heart when he realized what had happened. The wine barrel had split open and a stream
15 of good red wine was flowing past him into a field.

QUESTIONS
Your answer must not be more than 74 words.

1 What was the lorry carrying?
2 What did the driver suddenly see in front of him? Did he have to stop, or did he drive on? *(and)*
3 What slid off the back of the lorry at that moment? Did the man get out of the lorry, or did he carry on? *(but)*
4 Where did the barrel roll? What did it hit? *(and then)*
5 What woke up a beggar sleeping by the roadside?
6 What was flowing past him? Did this make him very happy, or did it make him very sad? *(and)*

39

By midday, the small party of boys, led by their school-master, had reached a height of 2500 feet. At this point the party had to stop climbing because one of the boys became seriously ill. The only thing the master could do
5 was to return to the mountain hut where they had spent the night. From there, he telephoned the police. As no rescue party could reach the boy quickly enough, the Royal Air Force Rescue Centre sent a helicopter with a policeman and a doctor on board. The helicopter soon
10 arrived on the scene, but the sides of the mountain were so steep that it could not land. A helicopter usually lands on four wheels, but it can land on two. However, the slope was too steep even for that. The pilot, therefore, kept the helicopter in the air with only one wheel
15 touching the mountain-side while the party carried the boy on board.

QUESTIONS
Your answer must not be more than 74 words.

1   How high up the mountain had the schoolmaster and the small party of boys climbed?
2   What happened to one of the boys at this point? What did the master do? *(so)*
3   What did he do from there? Did a helicopter quickly arrive on the scene or not? *(and)*
4   Was the mountain-side very steep or not? Could the pilot land on four wheels or not? Did he land on one wheel or not? *(and) (therefore)*
5   What did the party do then?

40

The local bank manager now regretted that he had offered to produce his play 'Business is Business'. As the first public performance was not far off, he was naturally getting anxious. He was having a difficult time because, of course, there were no professional actors in the town theatre group. In one amusing scene, the main character, a bank-clerk, had to greet an important customer who had just returned from a long voyage. (In real life, the bank-clerk was a baker, and the customer, a nurse from a nearby hospital). Dressed in a fur coat, the customer came on the stage and the bank-clerk sprang up from his desk waving his arms and saying 'This *is* a surprise!' 'Stop!' shouted the producer for the tenth time. 'She's a *customer,* not your mother-in-law! Remember you're a bank-clerk!'

This time, the poor baker lost his temper. 'Thank goodness I'm not!' he shouted. 'You ought to try being a baker some time!'

QUESTIONS
Your answer must not be more than 80 words.

1 Who had written the play 'Business is Business'?
  Who was producing it? *(not only . . . but . . . as well)*
2 Were the actors local people, or were they professional?
  Was the producer's work easy or difficult? *(and so)*
3 Who was the chief character in the play?
4 What was he in real life?
5 Whom did he have to greet? Did he do this well or badly? *(but)*
6 Did the producer stop him politely, or did he stop him rudely?
7 Did the bank-clerk get angry or not? Did he shout, 'You ought to try being a bank-clerk some time!' or did he shout, 'You ought to try being a baker some time!'? *(and)*

Chapter 3
The complex sentence

To the teacher

1   *AIMS*
(a) To enable the student to write complex sentences.
(b) To enable the student to put these sentences together to form a continuous paragraph.
(c) To give the student practice in writing continuous prose using conjunctions, adverbs, participles, gerunds, and connecting phrases.
(d) To provide revision practice in the writing of simple and compound sentences (learned in Chapters 1 and 2).
(e) To guide the student towards an elementary form of summary writing by providing him with specific information *(Points)* which should be joined together to form an orderly paragraph.

2   *HOW THE STUDENT SHOULD WORK*
This chapter has been divided into two parts, each consisting of ten passages. In both parts the student will be required to write complex sentences in a logical sequence. The method for doing this, however, will differ in each section.

(a) *Question and Answer*
The method that has been learned to date will again be employed in the first part of this Chapter (passages 41-50). Here the student will be required to write complex sentences by answering two or sometimes three questions *in a single sentence*. The conjunctions to be used are given in brackets.
Here is an example:
Did he open the door or not? What did he find? What had accidentally entered the room? *(On opening) (that) (and that)*
The answer would be given as *one* complex sentence:
On opening the door, he found that the window had been left open and that a bird had accidentally entered the room.

(b) *Word Order*
The student should be given to understand that each clause in a complex sentence usually keeps to the S/V/O pattern.
This is particularly obvious in indirect speech:

Subject	Verb	Object

			Subject	Verb	Object
He	said	that	he	would write	a letter

Even in a highly involved sentence, this pattern is followed:

			Subject	
Subject		Verb	Object	Qualifying Phrase
The beggar who		came	towards me	outside my house just as

Subject	Verb		Object
I	was getting ready		to open the gate

	Verb
would not go away	

		Object	
	Subject	Verb	Object
until	I	had given	him some money

When writing complex sentences students often find it difficult to decide when to insert a subject and when to leave it out. Sometimes they employ one subject too many, as in:

The man when he left the house he . . .
for *When the man* left the house he . . .

Or: The people who live next door they asked me . . .
for The people who live next door *asked* me . . .

At other times the subject is wrongly omitted:

When the man left the house forgot to lock . . .
for When the man left the house *he* forgot to lock . . .

Special attention should be paid to these difficulties.

3   *VOCABULARY RANGE*
The student's *passive* vocabulary should be about 1600 words. The actual range (taking into account the words used in the previous Chapters) is about 1400 words. The passages have been graded in order of increasing difficulty.

4   *LENGTH OF EACH PASSAGE*
About 230 words (maximum two paragraphs).

5   *LENGTH OF SUMMARIES*
Passages 41-50:   80-100 words.
Passages 51-60:   80 words.

6   *STRUCTURES*
All tenses active and passive. A reasonable working knowledge of most elementary structures has been assumed. The student will be expected to join sentences using participles and the gerund construction after prepositions.

The *conjunctions* which the student will be expected to use in this chapter are as follows: although/though, as, because, even, if/whether, hardly . . . when, since, so that . . . would, that (indirect speech), to/in order to, unless, until, when, where, which, while, who.

Connecting words and phrases: some time later, just after, in time, that evening, at first, rather than, a little later, after a time, after this, at last, only to + verb.

To the student

In this chapter you will learn how to use conjunctions to form *complex* sentences, that is, sentences which contain one main idea and one or more less important ideas. The chapter has been divided into two parts. Your way of working will differ in each part.

Before you begin each piece, read these instructions *very* carefully:

How to Work
1   Read the passage carefully two or three times.
2   Write a full answer to each question. When several questions are given together, join up your answers with the conjunctions or phrases given in brackets. Each answer you write must be *a complete sentence*.
3   Your answers to the questions must follow each other so that all your sentences will form *a complete paragraph*.
4   Read through your work and correct your mistakes.
5   Count the number of words in your paragraph. Do not go over the word limit. At the end of your paragraph write the number of words that you have used.
6   Give your paragraph a title.

Work through this example carefully and then try to do the exercises in the same way by yourself.

Example
    My neighbour's children love playing hide-and-seek as all children do, but no one expected that a game they played last week would be reported in the local newspaper.
    One afternoon, they were playing in the street just outside the
5   post-office. Young Ian, who is only five years old, found the perfect place to hide. His sister, Janet, had shut her eyes and was counting up to ten when Ian noticed that the small metal door of the letter-box had been left open. The postman had just taken all the letters out and had gone into the post-office
10 to see if there were any parcels. Ian climbed into the letter-box and pulled the door from the inside so hard that it locked. Soon realizing what he had done, he became very frightened and started crying. Meanwhile, Janet was looking for him everywhere but could not find him. It was lucky she happened
15 to stop outside the letter-box and hear her brother's cries. She immediately ran to tell the postman who hurried out to unlock the metal door. Ian was now free, but he had had such a bad

fright that he could not stop crying. The postman, however,
soon found a way of making him laugh again. He told him
20 that next time he wanted to hide in a letter-box, he should
remember to stick a stamp on himself!

QUESTIONS

Your answer must not be more than 80 words.

1 What were my neighbour's children playing outside the post-
office one afternoon?
2 Had the letter-box been left open or not? Where did young Ian
climb? Did he lock himself in or not? *(Finding that) (and)*
3 When did his sister, Janet, realize where he was hiding? What
did she do? *(so)*
4 How did the postman make Ian stop crying after he had let
him out? *(After letting . . . . by telling)*

ANSWER

A Strange 'Letter'

One afternoon my neighbour's children were playing hide-and-
seek outside the post-office. *Finding that* the letter-box had been
left open, young Ian climbed into it *and* locked himself in. His
sister, Janet, realized where he was hiding when she heard his cries
so she ran to tell the postman. *After* letting him out, the postman
made Ian stop crying *by telling* him that next time he wanted to
hide in a letter-box he should remember to stick a stamp on himself!

80 Words.

41

After having lived for over twenty years in the same district, Albert Hall was forced to move to a new neighbourhood. He surprised his landlord by telling him that he was leaving because he could not afford to buy any more chocolate.

5 It all began a year ago when Albert returned home one evening and found a large dog in front of his gate. He was very fond of animals and as he happened to have a small piece of chocolate in his pocket, he gave it to the dog. The next day, the dog was there again. It held up its paws and received another

10 piece of chocolate as a reward. Albert called his new friend 'Bingo'. He never found out the dog's real name, nor who his owner was. However, Bingo appeared regularly every afternoon and it was quite clear that he preferred chocolate to bones. He soon grew dissatisfied with small pieces of chocolate

15 and demanded a large bar a day. If at any time Albert neglected his duty, Bingo got very angry and refused to let him open the gate. Albert was now at Bingo's mercy and had to bribe him to get into his own house! He spent such a large part of his weekly wages to keep Bingo supplied with chocolate that

20 in the end he had to move somewhere else.

QUESTIONS

Your answer must not be more than 76 words.

1 What did Albert Hall see in front of his gate one evening? What did he give it? *(and)*
2 Did the dog become a regular visitor or not? What did Albert call it? *(and)*
3 What did Bingo demand in time?
4 What would he do if he did not receive any? *(If he . . . and . . .)*
5 Could Albert afford so much chocolate? Did he have to move to a new neighbourhood or not? *(Since Albert)*

42

It was years since I had visited my home town and I was determined to enjoy my stay. I went to see my old friend, Tom Clark who, among other things, was a member of the Local Council. At the time Tom was busy making arrangements for a dis-
5 tinguished writer to give a talk on modern literature at the town library. As the subject interested me a great deal, I gladly accepted Tom's invitation to go with him.

Tom was going to introduce the guest speaker and that evening we went to the library to meet him. Since he had not yet
10 arrived, I left Tom and went into the Reading Room where a large audience had already gathered. I was disappointed to find that I did not know a single person there. Just before the talk was due to begin, I saw Tom waving to me from the doorway. I went to him immediately, as he looked very
15 worried. He explained that he had just received a telephone message from the writer's secretary. Our guest speaker had missed the train and would be unable to come! While we were thinking about the problem, Tom suddenly asked me if I would mind acting as speaker. I hardly had time to think
20 about the matter when I found I was being led into the Reading Room to address the waiting audience!

QUESTIONS

Your answer must not be more than 86 words.

1 Whom did I go and see when I returned to my home town after many years' absence? *(On returning . . .)*
2 Whom had Tom invited to give a talk at the local library?
3 Did the subject interest me or not? Did he ask me to go with him? *(As the subject . . .)*
4 Who telephoned that evening just before the talk was about to begin? Would the speaker be able to come or not? *(That evening . . . to say that)*
5 Did Tom then suggest that I should address the audience or not? Where did he lead me? *(and)*

43

My friend Henry has a most unusual hobby. He likes planting
flowers in strange places. When spring comes round, you can
always tell that Henry has been about because the dirty sides
of canals, land covered with rubbish, and railway banks sud-
5 denly become full of flowers. In his spare time, with pockets
full of seeds, Henry goes round on his bicycle. He has a long
pipe with him to blow seeds into spots that are hard to reach.
When his flowers fade, he goes round again to collect their
seeds. In this way he always has a big supply.
10 Many people make fun of Henry, but he never lets himself get
upset. Recently I was having tea with him and he told me that
once he was planting seeds in a large piece of waste land when
the owner came along and sent him away. Henry returned some
days later when there was no one about. You can imagine how
15 surprised the owner was when, one day, he saw a large letter
'H' in flowers which went right across this neglected piece of
land! Henry took me round his house and I was astonished to
see that there was only one small bunch of flowers in a pot.
When I questioned him about this, he answered, 'They're not
20 fresh. They're artificial. Fresh flowers should be out there
where they belong.' And he pointed out of the window to a
garden full of flowers.

QUESTIONS
Your answer must not be more than 85 words.

1   What is Henry's hobby?
2   Does he go round on a bicycle in his spare time, or does he go
     round on foot? Why does he take a long pipe with him? *(and)*
3   Do people sometimes make fun of him or not? Can they ever
     prevent him from planting seeds in neglected pieces of land?
     (but)
4   Does Henry have real flowers in his own house, or does he have
     artificial ones? What does he believe? *(Even though he loves
     flowers so much . . . because)*

44

The whole family objected violently when my brother and I said we were going to spend our Christmas holidays abroad. Mother said that as there would be a family re-union party, we would have to be present. Though we always enjoyed these
5 occasions, nothing could persuade us to stay.

Two days before Christmas, we went to a small town in southern Germany. We spent the whole of Christmas Eve sight-seeing. There was so much activity in the town that it added to our excitement. The streets were crowded with people
10 and the shops were full of wonderful things. In the evening, we went to listen to Christmas songs sung by children round the brightly lit tree in the main square. We returned to our hotel late that night, greatly looking forward to the next day when we planned to have a meal at the best restaurant in town. But
15 in the morning the streets were deserted. To make matters worse, all the shops—including the restaurants—were shut. We searched in vain for hours and at last had to return to our hotel feeling very miserable. Our Christmas 'feast' was a bag of fruit which my brother had happened to buy the day before.
20 Our thoughts sadly turned to home where, at that moment, the whole family must have been wishing us a 'Merry Christmas'.

QUESTIONS
Your answer must not be more than 94 words.

1   Did the whole family want us to stay at home for Christmas or not? Where did my brother and I go? *(In spite of the fact that)*
2   When did we go sight-seeing?
3 . Where did we go in the evening? Why? *(In the evening . . . to . . .)*
4   Where did we intend to eat next day? Did we search for hours or not? Did we find everything shut or open? Where did we return? *(but after searching . . . so . . .)*
5   What did we eat? How did we feel when we thought of every-one at home? *(and)*

45

As it came near the corner, the taxi stopped suddenly. The driver got out looking very puzzled. A big lorry which had been following the taxi stopped too. The taxi driver was now standing at the corner looking up at the sky and the lorry driver
5 went and joined him. A number of cars behind were forced to stop as well and soon a large crowd of people had gathered at the corner.

The cause of all this trouble was a very strange noise. It sounded as if thousands and thousands of birds were singing
10 together. The noise was quite frightening and many people looked disturbed. The most extraordinary thing was that, apart from one or two pigeons, there was not a bird in sight. No one was able to solve the mystery, until two policemen arrived. They noticed a large advertisement for a film high up
15 on a wall nearby. As the noise seemed to be coming from this direction, they climbed up and found that a tape-recorder had been hidden behind the advertisement. The noise made by birds singing was being broadcast over powerful loudspeakers so as to attract the attention of passers-by. The police asked the
20 advertisers to take the recorder away because the advertisement had attracted so much attention that it was impossible for a great many cars and buses to move freely in the street.

QUESTIONS
Your answer must not be more than 82 words.

1 Where did a large crowd gather after the traffic stopped?
2 Did everyone look puzzled or not? Could thousands of birds be heard singing or not? Were there many in sight? *(because)* *(though there were hardly any)*
3 What did two policemen see high up on a wall? *(Then)*
4 Did they climb up or not? How had the noise been caused? Where was it hidden? *(After climbing)* *(they found that)* *(which)*
5 What did the police ask the advertisers to do? Had the loud noise stopped the traffic or not? *(because)*

46

Dark black clouds in a dull sky meant one thing and one thing
only: there was going to be a thunderstorm. Not one of us had
brought an umbrella, or even a raincoat, so when Jack suggested we should go to a museum, we all agreed immediately.
5 As we had been shopping all morning and were now feeling
very tired, it would be a pleasure to sit down. We took a
bus and arrived just as large drops of rain were beginning
to fall.
The museum was quite deserted and very peaceful. We sat
10 down in the main hall and listened to the rain beating against
the windows. Suddenly there was a great disturbance at the
entrance. Then a large party of school-boys were led in by a
teacher. The poor man was trying to keep them quiet and
threatening to punish them, but they did not pay the slightest
15 attention. The boys ran here and there like a wild tribe.
Apologizing for this lack of discipline, the teacher explained
that the boys were 'rather excited'. But in the end the noise
proved too much for us and we decided to leave. As Jack
remarked when we were walking in the rain, the boys had more
20 right to be in the museum than we had. After all, they had
come on an 'educational' visit, while we had simply wanted to
get out of the rain.

QUESTIONS
Your answer must not be more than 78 words.

1 Was there going to be a thunderstorm or not? Did we have
  umbrellas and raincoats with us? Where did we decide to go?
  (and as)
2 When did it begin raining?
3 Was it very quiet in the main hall or not? Who came in? *(At
  first . . . until . . .)*
4 Who was in charge of them? Could he keep order? *(but)*
5 What did we prefer to do rather than put up with so much
  noise? *(Rather than . . .)*

47

Old Sally Gibbs was a very strange woman. The fine house in
which she had lived overlooked a lovely valley. But she
hardly ever went out. Though a servant looked after her, her
only real companions were two cats. For years she had refused
5 to see any of her relations as she felt that all they were interested
in was her money.
In this she was right. After her death, the few relations she
had, gathered at the house to hear Sally's lawyer read her will.
They were all sure that Sally had left a great fortune and they
10 each demanded a share. This led to violent arguments. In
particular, they quarrelled about the house. Sally's nephew
felt that it should go to him as he was one of the few people
who used to visit his old aunt before she cut herself off from
her relations. Sally's cousin objected to this and there was an
15 angry scene in the living-room while they waited for the
lawyer to arrive. When the lawyer entered, the nephew said
jokingly that his aunt had probably left hundreds of debts.
The lawyer did not even smile at this and asked them all to sit
down. He began to read the will in a solemn voice. Sally had
20 indeed been immensely rich – but she had left the whole of her
fortune to her two cats!

QUESTIONS
Your answer must not be more than 88 words.

1   Did Sally Gibbs wish to see any of her relations while she was
     alive or not? With whom did she prefer to live? *(preferring)*
2   Why did her relations come to her house after her death?
3   Did they think she had left them a great deal of money or not?
     Did they quarrel violently among themselves just before the
     lawyer entered or not? *(Thinking that . . .)*
4   What did they learn when the will was read out? *(However)*

48

An old friend from abroad, whom I was expecting to stay with
me, telephoned from the airport to tell me that he had arrived.
I was still at the office at the time, but I had made arrangements
for his arrival. After explaining where my new flat was, I
5　told him that I had left the key under the door-mat. As I was
likely to be home rather late, I advised him to go into the
kitchen and help himself to food and drink.

Two hours later my friend telephoned me from the flat. At
the moment, he said, he was listening to some of my records
10　after having just had a truly wonderful meal. He had found a
pan on the gas stove and fried two eggs and had helped himself to some cold chicken from the refrigerator. Now, he said,
he was drinking a glass of orange juice and he hoped I would
join him. When I asked him if he had reached the flat without
15　difficulty, he answered that he had not been able to find the
key under the door-mat, but fortunately the living-room
window just by the apple tree had been left open and he had
climbed in. I listened to all this in astonishment. There is no
apple tree in front of my living-room, but there is one in front
20　of my neighbour's!

QUESTIONS
Your answer must not be more than 96 words.

1　Where was I when my friend arrived from abroad? Did I
　　tell him how to get to my flat or not? *(so)*
2　Where did I tell him the key was? What would he find in the
　　kitchen? *(and)*
3　Who rang up some time later? Had he had a fine meal or not?
　　(to say that)
4　Was the key under the door-mat or not? Had he got into the
　　flat through the living-room window by the apple tree, or had
　　he got in through the back door? *(As the key . . .)*
5　How did I feel when I heard this? Whose flat had my friend
　　entered? *(because)*

49

It had been a tiring day and I was looking forward to a quiet
evening. My husband would not be back until late and I had
decided to settle down in a comfortable armchair in the living-
room and read a book. I put the children to bed early and
5 prepared a cold supper and some coffee. Soon I was sitting
comfortably with a tray full of food before me and a book at
my side.

I was just beginning to eat when the telephone rang. I dropped
my knife and fork and hurried to answer it. By the time I
10 got back to the living-room, my coffee had got cold. After I
finished my supper, I began drinking cold coffee with my book
open at page one. Suddenly there was a loud knock at the door.
It gave me such a surprise that I spilt the coffee and made an
ugly stain on my skirt. Some stranger had lost his way and
15 wanted me to direct him. It took me ages to get rid of him. At
length I managed to sit down again and actually read a whole
page without further interruption – until the baby woke up.
He began crying loudly and I rushed upstairs. The baby was
still awake at 11 o'clock when my husband came home. I
20 could have screamed when he asked me if I had spent a
pleasant evening!

QUESTIONS
Your answer must not be more than 98 words.

1   What did the writer prepare after she had put the children to
    bed? *(After putting . . .)*
2   Would her husband be home early or late? How did she
    intend to spend the evening? *(As her husband . . .)*
3   What happened just as she was beginning to eat?
4   Did she have time to sit down again or not? Who knocked at
    the door? *(She hardly . . . when . . .)*
5   Did she begin reading when he had left or not? Why did she
    have to stop? *(but . . . because . . .)*
6   What did her husband ask her when he returned at 11 o'clock?
    Was the baby still awake, or was it asleep? *(On returning . . .
    even though . . .)*

50

Now that smoking is considered to be very dangerous to the
health, it is especially difficult for children to buy cigarettes or
tobacco. Our tobacconist, Mr Soames, has always been very
careful about this. If his customers are very young, he always
5 asks them whom the cigarettes are for.
One day, a little girl whom he had never seen before walked
boldly into his shop and demanded twenty cigarettes. She had
the exact amount of money in her hand and seemed very sure
of herself. Mr Soames was so surprised by her confident
10 manner that he forgot to ask his usual question. Instead, he
asked her what kind of cigarettes she wanted. The girl replied
promptly and handed him the money. While he was giving her
the cigarettes, Mr Soames said laughingly that as she was so
young she should hide the packet in her pocket in case a
15 policeman saw it. However, the little girl did not seem to
find this very funny. Without even smiling she took the packet
and walked towards the door. Suddenly she stopped, turned
round, and looked steadily at Mr Soames. There was a
moment's deathly silence and the tobacconist wondered what
20 she was going to say. All at once, in a clear, solemn voice, the
girl declared, 'My dad *is* a policeman,' and with that she walked
quickly out of the shop.

QUESTIONS
Your answer must not be more than 83 words.

1 Does our tobacconist, Mr Soames, ever sell cigarettes to
children? What does he first ask them? (. . . *never* . . .
without asking . . .)
2 Why did he forget to do so when a young girl demanded a
packet of cigarettes? *(because)*
3 Where did he advise her to hide the packet? Why? *(However)*
(so that . . . would not)
4 Was the girl amused by this or not? What did she tell him just
as she was leaving the shop? *(and)*

To the teacher

HOW THE STUDENT SHOULD WORK

In the remaining part of this chapter, there is a departure from the 'question and answer' technique which the student has employed so far. The student will still be provided with conjunctions so that he can write complex sentences. But here he has been given note form 'answers' to imaginary questions which he will join up to make a summary. These note form 'answers' are, in fact, the main *Points* of a precis. When writing his summary, the student may refer to the passage if he wishes.

To the student

The exercises that follow are slightly different from those you have done so far. There are no questions to answer in these exercises: the 'questions' have been answered for you in note form. You will be asked to put the notes together (using the conjunctions given) so as to make a paragraph.

Before you begin each piece, read these instructions *very* carefully:

How to Work

1 Read the passage carefully two or three times.
2 Read the instructions below each passage which will tell you what you will have to do. Under these instructions you will find a list of *Points* which have been written in note form. Using the conjunctions given at the side, join up these points to make sentences. The number of points which each sentence will contain is given in brackets. Your sentences should form *a complete paragraph.*
3 Read through your work and correct your mistakes.
4 Count the number of words in your paragraph. Do not go over the word limit. At the end of your paragraph, write the number of words that you have used.
5 Give your paragraph a title.

Work through this example carefully, then try to do the exercises in the same way by yourself.

Example

Forty-two horses had taken up their positions on the starting line for the greatest race of the season. The course was extremely difficult and few horses were expected to finish. All eyes were on the favourites, College Boy and Sweet Seventeen.

5 Both horses had won a great many races in the past and they had equal chances of winning now.

Though the horses got off to a good start, it was not long before over half of them were out of the race. As was expected, College Boy and Sweet Seventeen had got well in front with
10 the remaining horses grouped together some way behind. On a sharp corner, three of the horses leading the group fell, throwing the riders behind into great confusion. As the race progressed, the track became full of horses without riders. Towards the end, there were only three horses left: College
15 Boy and Sweet Seventeen were still leading with an unknown horse, Tom Thumb, a very long way behind. The crowd was very disappointed when on the last jump in the race, the riders of both favourite horses failed to keep in the saddle. Everyone roared with delight when College Boy continued by himself and
20 'won' the race—without his rider! Tom Thumb now took his time and the crowd cheered and applauded as he crossed the finishing line without a rival in sight.

INSTRUCTIONS

In not more than 80 *words* describe what happened from the moment the horses set off to the end of the race.

POINTS	CONNECTIONS
[1] Race began.	*As soon as*
[2] Favourites, C. Boy, S. Seventeen ahead.	
[3] Bend—riders over.	*On*
[4] Horses following—out of race.	*and*
[5] Three left: favourites, unknown.	*Towards the end*
[6] Riders fell.	*However*
[7] C. Boy 'won'—by himself.	*though*
[8] T. Thumb alone—real winner.	*Since*

ANSWER

An Exciting Race

As soon as the race began, the favourites, College Boy and Sweet Seventeen, went ahead. *On* a dangerous bend a few riders went over *and* most of the horses following fell out of the race. *Towards the end,* there were only three left: the favourites and an unknown horse, Tom Thumb. However, the riders of both favourites fell too, *though* College Boy continued by himself and 'won'. *Since* Tom Thumb was now on his own, he became the real winner.

80 Words.

51

As the plane circled over the airport, everyone sensed that something was wrong. The plane was moving unsteadily through the air, and although the passengers had fastened their seat belts, they were suddenly thrown forward. At that moment,
5 the air-hostess appeared. She looked very pale, but was quite calm. Speaking quickly but almost in a whisper, she informed everyone that the pilot had fainted and asked if any of the passengers knew anything about machines – or at least how to drive a car. After a moment's hesitation, a man got up and
10 followed the hostess into the pilot's cabin.
Moving the pilot aside, the man took his seat and listened carefully to the urgent instructions that were being sent by radio from the airport below. The plane was now dangerously close to the ground, but to everyone's relief, it soon began
15 to climb. The man had to circle the airport several times in order to become familiar with the controls. But the danger had not yet passed. The terrible moment came when he had to land. Following instructions, the man guided the plane towards the airfield. It shook violently as it touched the ground and
20 then moved rapidly across the field, but after a long run it stopped safely. Outside, a crowd of people who had been watching anxiously, rushed forward to congratulate the 'pilot' on a perfect landing.

INSTRUCTIONS
In not more than 80 words, describe what happened after the passenger followed the hostess into the pilot's cabin.

POINTS   *CONNECTIONS*
[1] Moved pilot, passenger sat down.]   *When he . . .*
[2] Listened instructions – radio – below.]   *and . . . which . . .*
[3] Plane dangerously low – climbed.]   *Though*
[4] Round airport several times.]   *and*
[5] Instructions – airfield.]   *Then, acting on*
[6] Touched ground, shook violently.]   *On . . .*
[7] Moved rapidly, stopped safely.]   *then . . . until . . .*
[8] Anxious crowd – congratulate 'pilot'.]   *After this*

52

Our local inn, 'The Red Lion', is a very old building. The ancient brick walls are covered with plaster and supported by heavy wooden beams. All the windows are made up of small squares of glass held together by thin strips of lead. The
5 owner is a cheerful fellow who loves collecting strange ornaments and his inn is almost like a museum inside. Hanging on the walls there are guns, swords, bows, arrows, and numerous weapons of various types.

Recently there has been a new addition. The inn-keeper
10 bought a very curious object from one of his customers: a Victorian musical instrument. It can best be described as a large music-box. This piece of furniture is over six feet tall and there is a small window at the top through which can be seen a number of wheels with small metal teeth. As soon as
15 the instrument is wound up by means of a handle at the side, the wheels go round and play three charming little tunes. As the bell-like tunes are very faint, you have to listen carefully to hear them. But what a pleasant change it is from the noisy music that can be heard in so many inns nowadays! The
20 old-fashioned music-box has caused a lot of excitement in our village and has already attracted a large number of visitors.

INSTRUCTIONS
Make a summary of the passage from line 4 ('The owner . . .') to the end *in not more than 80 words.*

POINTS	*CONNECTIONS*
[1] Owner, local inn – large collection strange objects.	*who*
[2] Recently bought Victorian musical instrument from customer.	
[3] Like large music-box.	*Over six feet tall, it . . .*
[4] Window at top – has wheels behind it.	*There is . . . which . . .*
[5] Go round when wound up.	*These*
[6] Play three tunes.	*and*
[7] Attracted many visitors.	*Because it is so unusual . . .*

53

We were about to gather up our belongings and return to our car when a man appeared. He looked very annoyed indeed and asked us angrily if we realized that these grounds were private property. Father looked very confused and the man pointed to
5 a notice which said that camping was strictly forbidden. Poor father explained that he had not seen the notice and did not know that camping was not allowed. Though father apologized, the man did not seem satisfied and asked him for his name and address. All the way home, we were so upset that hardly any-
10 one spoke a word. This unpleasant event had spoilt a wonderful day in the country.
For the rest of the week, we wondered what would happen. The following Sunday, we stayed at home even though it was a fine day. About noon, a large and very expensive car stopped
15 outside our house. We were astonished when we saw several people preparing to have a picnic in our small garden. Father got very angry and went out to ask them what they thought they were doing. You can imagine his surprise when he recognized the man who had taken our address the week
20 before! Both men burst out laughing and father welcomed the strangers into the house. In time, we became good friends— but we learned a lesson we have never forgotten.

INSTRUCTIONS
In not more than 80 words describe what happened after the man pointed out that camping was forbidden.

POINTS		*CONNECTIONS*
[1]	Father explained – camping forbidden.	*Although . . . that . .*
[2]	Man not satisfied, took name and address.	*and*
[3]	Went home – upset.	*We all*
[4]	Following Sunday – midday.	
[5]	Large car outside house.	
[6]	Several strangers – picnic – garden.	*and*
[7]	Father angry – laughed – recognized.	*but . . . when . . .*
[8]	Week before – invited strangers – house.	*whom . . . and . . .*

54

Silas Minton's funeral was a quiet affair. It was attended by the only relations he had in the world, his niece and nephew, and by a few friends. The priest who had travelled over a hundred miles into this wild part of the country was now
5 getting ready for the simple ceremony. Minton, or 'Minty' as his friends used to call him, had led a hard life looking for gold in a lonely part of Western Australia. He had always refused to work in a gold mine because he believed that he could do better on his own. Although he was not a boastful
10 person, he had often declared that one day he would find a lump of gold as big as his head and with that he would retire and live in comfort for the rest of his life. But his dreams of great wealth never came true. For many years he had hardly earned enough money to keep himself alive.
15 Two men now gently lifted the rough wooden box that contained Minty's body, but they almost dropped it when they heard a loud cry from the grave-digger. His spade had struck something hard in the rocky soil and he was shouting excitedly. Then he held up a large stone. Though it was covered with dirt,
20 the stone shone curiously in the fierce sunlight: it was unmistakably a heavy piece of solid gold!

INSTRUCTIONS
Write a summary of the passage from line 5 ('Minton . . . ') to the end *in not more than 80 words.*

POINTS   *CONNECTIONS*

[1] Worked on his own – gold digger – West ⎤ *Silas Minton had*
     Australia.   ⎦

[2] Sure he would find a lot of gold.   ⎤ *Though*
[3] Failed, lived in poverty.   ⎦ *and*
[4] Funeral – friends – bury him.   ⎤ *Now*
[5] Surprised – grave-digger shouting.   ⎦ *They . . . when . . .*
[6] Spade – something hard.   ⎤ *His*
[7] Held up object – looked like stone.   │ *and . . . which . . .*
[8] Turned out to be – gold.   ⎦ *but which*

55

We were losing the battle. Our King was old and weak and could hardly move. He was hiding just outside the castle walls. Of the three soldiers who had been appointed to protect him, two had been killed while on duty and I was left alone.

5 From where I was standing, I had a good view of the battle. Fortunately for us, our Queen was a young and active woman. Tall, dark, and very beautiful, she looked splendid out there in the battle-field with her knights at her side. She had fought with great courage and already killed two enemy officers
10 herself. Since we had lost so many men it was difficult for her to attack. She therefore decided to do all she could to defend the king. I got a shock when I saw a humble enemy soldier threatening her! He came up very close, but her brave knights sacrificed their lives to save her. Alone now, she was
15 trapped by the enemy, and though she fought hard, she, too, lost her life. Great numbers of enemy officers and soldiers now descended upon us and soon destroyed the castle. Completely defeated, the King and I tried to run away together, but it was too late. As the King moved up behind me, I heard
20 the words 'Check mate'. Another game of chess had come to an end.

INSTRUCTIONS

Write a summary in the third person of the 'soldier's' account of the 'battle' *in not more than 80 words*.

POINTS   CONNECTIONS

[1] King hiding – castle.
[2] One soldier – defend him.   *with*
[3] Queen – fought bravely.   *Meanwhile*
[4] Two enemy officers.   *and*
[5] Soldier threatened.   *When*
[6] Knights gave up lives.
[7] Queen – trapped – fought hard – killed.   *Now alone . . . but*
                                         although
[8] Enemy attacked – destroyed castle.   *After this . . . and*
[9] Soldier and King escape.   *While*
[10] King killed. Game of chess.   *thus ending*

56

It was very hot in the small court-room and everybody was feeling sleepy. After a tiring morning, the clerks were anxious to get off to lunch and even the judge must have felt relieved when the last case came up before the court. A short, middle-
5 aged man with grey hair and small blue eyes was now standing before him. The man had a foolish expression on his face and he kept looking around stupidly as if he was trying hard to understand what was going on.

The man was accused of breaking into a house and stealing a
10 cheap watch. The witness who was called did not give a very clear account of what had happened. He claimed to have seen a man outside the house one night, but on being questioned further, he confessed that he was not sure whether this was the man. The judge considered the matter for a short time
15 and then declared that as there was no real proof, the man could not be found guilty of any crime. He said that the case was dismissed and then rose to go. Meanwhile, the accused looked very puzzled. It was clear that he had not understood a thing. Noticing this, the judge paused for a moment and then
20 the man said suddenly, 'Excuse me, sir, but do I have to give the watch back or not?'

INSTRUCTIONS
Write a summary of the passage from line 4 ('A short . . ') to the end *in not more than 80 words.*

POINTS		*CONNECTIONS*
[1]	Standing before judge.	*who*
[2]	Kept looking around stupidly.	
[3]	Accused – watch.	*He*
[4]	Witness not sure – really thief.	*but*
[5]	Clear proof.	*In the absence*
[6]	Dismissed case.	
[7]	Judge preparing to leave.	*While*
[8]	Not understood.	*who*
[9]	Asked – return watch.	*whether*

57

People are very careless with money. One occasionally hears that pet dogs or even small children have 'eaten' bank notes. Goats are supposed to be particularly fond of them. Many expensive fires have been lit with precious bundles of notes
5 hidden up chimneys. In this respect, banks are a great blessing because we no longer have to hide money in places where it can easily be destroyed or stolen. However, accidents still happen—as I found to my cost recently.

I gave my housekeeper an old pair of trousers to wash and
10 went into the study to read. My housekeeper usually goes through my pockets before washing anything, but for some reason she failed to do so on this occasion. As I was reading, I suddenly remembered that there was a five pound note in the back pocket of the pair of trousers I had given her. I dropped
15 my book and rushed into the bathroom. But it was too late. My housekeeper told me that my trousers had been in the washing-machine for ten minutes already! I stopped the machine and pulled out my trousers as quickly as possible. I nearly burnt my fingers trying to unbutton my back pocket.
20 At last I managed to find the wet piece of paper which had once been a five pound note. To my great disappointment, I discovered that it was pure white!

INSTRUCTIONS

In not more than 80 words describe what happened from the moment the writer gave his trousers to the housekeeper.

POINTS		CONNECTIONS
[1]	Gave old pair of trousers—to wash.	*The writer*
[2]	Went to study.	*and*
[3]	Remembered note—back pocket.	*After a time . . .*
		which
[4]	Rushed bathroom.	*He*
[5]	Washing-machine—10 minutes.	*only to learn*
[6]	Stopped machine.	*Then*
[7]	Pulled out trousers.	
[8]	Unbuttoned pocket.	*and*
[9]	Found note—white.	*At last . . . which*

58

The guard went through carriage after carriage inquiring whether there was a doctor on the train. He found one at last and quickly led him to the luggage-van where a tall man was lying on the floor stretched out among heaps of mail-bags with
5   a cushion under his head. The guard explained that he had discovered the man in the passage and finding that he was seriously ill, had dragged him into the luggage-van. The doctor loosened the man's collar and after examining him thoroughly, told the guard that the man was unconscious and
10 would have to be taken to hospital. When he heard this, the guard answered that the express train could not be stopped without first informing the station-master of the main-line station which was nearly fifty miles away. Meanwhile, the man's condition gradually got worse.
15 There seemed to be no way of sending a message until the guard had the idea of throwing a note on to the platform of a small village station as the train flashed past. Fortunately, someone picked the note up and telephoned the main-line station. This was a strange way of sending a message, but it
20 worked. Shortly afterwards, the train was stopped for a few minutes at a small village station several miles further on so that the sick man could be taken to hospital.

INSTRUCTIONS

Describe what happened during the journey after the guard explained how he had dragged the sick man into the luggage-van. *Do not use more than 80 words.*

POINTS		*CONNECTIONS*
[1]	Loosened collar – examined.]	*After loosening*
[2]	Unconscious – hospital.	*He realized . . .*
		and . . .
[3]	Express – not stop.	*However*
[4]	Main-line station informed.	*unless*
[5]	Passed village station.	*As the train*
[6]	Note – platform.	
[7]	Picked up, sent.	*This . . . and . . .*
[8]	Stopped.	*A little later*
[9]	Taken hospital.	*and*

59

On my last day in Nairobi, I decided to visit the game reserve. Leaving my hotel, I bought a map and hired a car. On the way I stopped to take photographs of many interesting animals. A little later, I was delighted when I saw notices saying:
5 'Caution: Lions. Stay in Your Car.' I did not intend to get out and drove across a shallow stream. I was half-way across when my wheels began to spin: the car had stuck in the mud! Cursing my bad luck, I looked around carefully. There was not a lion in sight. I was soon in the stream and my clothes
10 got into a terrible state but there was nothing I could do. Though there was a forest quite near, I did not fancy the idea of going there. When I got back into the car, I felt very miserable. I wondered how long it would be before I was discovered by wild beasts. Elephants would not need a tin-
15 opener to provide the lions with a tasty meal of fresh human being! I was greatly relieved when, several hours later, a keeper drove up in a jeep and soon pulled my car on to dry land. It took me some time to explain my appearance when I returned to the hotel, but I do not think that anyone really
20 believed me.

INSTRUCTIONS
In not more than 80 words give an account of the writer's experiences while he was on the game reserve.

POINTS		*CONNECTIONS*
[1]	Took photographs – animals.	*After having*
[2]	Saw notice – lions.	*the writer . . .*
		which . . .
[3]	Drove – stream.	*While*
[4]	Car stuck.	
[5]	Looked round – no lions – got out.	*He . . . and as . . .*
[6]	Clothes – not move car.	*His . . . but . . .*
[7]	Got back in, waited hours.	*At last . . . and . . .*
[8]	Keeper arrived – jeep.	*until*
[9]	Car pulled out.	*and*

60

Some time ago, scientists began experiments to find out
whether it would be possible to set up a 'village' under the sea.
A five room 'house' was built in a garage work-shop and
lowered into the water off Port Sudan in the Red Sea. For 29
5   days, five men lived at a depth of 40 feet. At a much lower level,
two more divers stayed for a week in a smaller 'house'. On
returning to the surface, the men said that they had experienced
no difficulty in breathing and had made many interesting
scientific observations. The leader of the party, Commander
10 Cousteau, spoke of the possibility of cultivating the sea bed.
He said that if permanent stations were set up under the sea,
underwater farms could provide food for the growing popu-
lation of the world.

The divers in both 'houses' spent most of their time exploring
15 the depths of the sea. On four occasions they went down to
360 feet and observed many extraordinary forms of sea life,
some of which have never been seen before. It is possible to
move rapidly under the water in a special vessel known as a
'diving saucer'. During their stay, Commander Cousteau and
20 the diver Andre Falco reached a depth of 1000 feet and wit-
nessed a gathering of an immense colony of crabs which
numbered perhaps hundreds of millions.

INSTRUCTIONS
In not more than 80 words, describe how the divers spent their time
under the sea.

POINTS   *CONNECTIONS*
[1]   Five divers – 29 days – house.   ⎫
[2]   40 feet under sea.   ⎬ *at a depth*
[3]   Another two – week – house – deeper level. ⎭ *Meanwhile*
[4]   Explored depths.   ⎫
[5]   360 feet four times.   ⎬ *and as*
[6]   Saw strange forms sea life.   ⎭
[7]   Cousteau and Falco – saucer – 1000 feet. ⎫ *During their stay*
[8]   Millions of crabs.   ⎭ *where*

Chapter 4
Comprehension Precis and Composition

To the teacher

1 *AIMS*
(a) To enable the student to apply all that he has learned about sentence structure and word order.
(b) To enable the student to join sentences with conjunctions, participles etc. unaided.
(c) To test the student's understanding of the text (comprehension).
(d) To provide the student with practice in explaining words and phrases as they are used in the text (vocabulary).
(e) To enable the student to distinguish between essential and inessential material so that he will be able to write a précis on his own.
(f) To provide practice in writing simple essays which, in this chapter, take the form of continuation or reproduction exercises.

2 *HOW THE STUDENT SHOULD WORK*
This chapter has been divided into two parts, each consisting of ten passages. Each passage is just over 350 words in length and consists of three paragraphs. For the most part, comprehension and vocabulary questions are confined to the first two paragraphs; précis exercises to the last paragraph. The method for writing précis differs slightly in each part of the chapter.

(a) *Comprehension*
The student should be trained to give a short answer to each question *in one complete sentence*. This means that part of the question must be incorporated in each answer. If, for instance, the question is 'Why did the man return to the hotel?' the answer should not be 'Because he had forgotten his coat', but: 'The man returned to the hotel because he had forgotten his coat.' Students have a tendency to ignore tenses when answering questions. They should therefore be taught to distinguish clearly between present and past.

(b) *Vocabulary*
Dictionary definitions should *not* be given. Words should be explained *as they are used in the text* either by means of synonyms

or phrases. The student should be trained to replace the word in the text with the word or phrase he has chosen to see if it fits into the context. Only *one* explanation should be given for each word or phrase.

(c) *Precis*

In the first ten passages there is a return to the 'question and answer' technique, but with one important difference. The student should give note form answers to the questions in order to get his *points*. He should then join the points together to write his précis, referring to the passage if necessary. The purpose of the square brackets at the side of the questions is to help the student to join up his answers. They may, however, be ignored. Conjunctions etc. are not given in this chapter and must be supplied by the student. The number of words should be clearly written at the end of each précis. Articles, pronouns, etc. and compound words count as *single* words. A précis may be written in fewer than the required number of words, but on no account should the set limit be exceeded.

(d) *Essay-writing*

The student should be encouraged to write *within* his vocabulary range without the aid of a dictionary. As the titles are closely based on the passages, the student should use as many as he can of the words and phrases which are employed in the text. Essays should be limited to two or three paragraphs. At this stage, more emphasis should be placed on correct English than on subject-matter and the orderly presentation of ideas.

3 VOCABULARY RANGE

The student's *passive* vocabulary should be in the region of 2000 words. A further 400 words have been added to the *actual* range, bringing the total up to 1800 words.

4 STRUCTURES

A reasonable working knowledge of all the more common structures has been assumed. Highly involved sentences and unfamiliar constructions have been avoided.

To the student

In this chapter you will be applying all you have learned about simple, compound, and complex sentences. You will now be doing exercises in comprehension, vocabulary, précis, and essay writing.

How to Work

1 Read each passage carefully two or three times.

2 *Comprehension*
   In this type of exercise you will be asked to answer questions so that your teacher can see if you have understood the passage.

(a) After you have read the question, find the answer in the passage.

(b) Write a short answer *in one complete sentence* to each question.

(c) Use your own words as far as possible.

(d) In each answer use the same verb tense that is used in the question.

(e) Work neatly; number each answer carefully.

3 *Vocabulary*
   In this exercise you will be asked to explain words and phrases. You may use a phrase to explain a word if necessary. Explain each word and phrase *as it is used in the passage*.

(a) You will find a line reference after each word. Go back to the passage and note how the word has been used.

(b) Find a word or phrase of your own which could be used *in its place*.

(c) Do not give more than one explanation for each word or phrase.

4 *Precis*
   In this exercise you will be required to write a summary of a part of each passage. In the second half of Chapter 3 you will remember that you were given the *points* and asked to join them up. Here you will be expected to find the points yourself.

(a) Read the instructions which will tell you where your précis should begin and end, and exactly what you will have to do.

(b) Read again the part of the passage that you will have to summarize.

(c) Answer each question *in note form* to get your *points*.

(d) You will find brackets at the side of the questions. These show you how the answers may be joined to form sentences, but you will have to use connections of your own. You may disregard the brackets if you wish and join the points in your own way.

(e) When joining your points, you may refer to the passage if necessary, but try to use *your own words*. Your answer should be in one paragraph.

(f) Read through your work and correct your mistakes.

(g) At the end of your précis write the number of words you have used. You may write fewer than 80 words, but you must not go above the word limit.

(h) Give your précis a title.

5   *Essay*

The titles given are based on the passages. When writing an essay *do not* refer to a dictionary. Use as many as you can of the words and phrases that are employed in the passage.

Carefully work through the example given below and note how each question has been answered.

Example

Hidden passengers travelling in ships, trains, or even cars can be a terrible nuisance–especially when they are insects. In this respect there is a great difference between human beings and insects. The former make every possible effort to
5   avoid discovery, while the latter quickly draw attention to themselves.

We can only sympathize with the unfortunate man who had to stop his car soon after setting out from a country village to drive to London. Hearing a strange noise from the back of the
10 car, he naturally got out to have a look. He examined the wheels carefully but as he found nothing wrong, he continued his way. The noise began almost immediately and now it was louder than ever. Quickly turning his head, the man saw what appeared to be a great black cloud following the car. When he
15 stopped at a village further on, he was told that a queen bee must be hidden in his car as there were thousands of bees nearby.

On learning this, the man realized that the only way to escape would be to drive away as quickly as possible. After an hour's
20 hard driving, he arrived in London where he parked his car

outside a hotel and went in to have a drink. It was not long
before a customer who had seen him arrive hurried in to
inform him that his car was covered with bees. The poor
motorist telephoned the police and explained what had hap-
25 pened. The police decided that the best way to deal with the
situation would be to call a bee-keeper. In a short time, the
bee-keeper arrived. He found the unwelcome passenger hidden
near the wheels at the back of the car. Very grateful to the
motorist for this unexpected gift, the keeper took the queen
30 and her thousands of followers home in a large box. Equally
grateful, the motorist drove away in peace, at last free from
the 'black cloud' which had hung over his car.

1 *COMPREHENSION*
   Give short answers to these questions in your own words as
   far as possible. Use one complete sentence for each answer.
(a) How do human beings differ from insects when they hide in
   ships, trains, or cars?
(b) Why did the man stop his car soon after he had set out from a
   country village to drive to London?
(c) What did the man see on turning his head?

2 *VOCABULARY*
   Give another word or phrase to replace the following words
   as they are used in the passage: terrible (1.2); especially (1.2);
   avoid (1.5); discovery (1.5); sympathize (1.7); unfortunate (1.7);
   immediately (1.12).

3 *PRECIS*
   In not more than 80 words describe what happened after the
   motorist learnt that a queen bee must be hidden in his car.
   Use your own words as far as possible. Do not include anything
   that is not in the last paragraph.

   Answer these questions in note form to get your points.

[1] What did the man do to escape the bees?
[2] Where did he arrive?
[3] What did he do there?
[4] What did a customer tell him?
[5] Whom did the motorist telephone?
[6] Whom did they send?
[7] Where did he find the queen bee?
[8] What did the bee-keeper do with the queen and her followers?
[9] What did the motorist do then?

4   *ESSAY*
Write a composition in about 200 words on *one* of the following:
(a) Imagine that the bee-keeper did not arrive. Describe what the motorist did.
(b) Write a story about a person who hides in a life-boat on board a big ship.

POSSIBLE ANSWERS
1   *COMPREHENSION*
(a) When they hide in ships, trains, or cars human beings do all they can to avoid being found, while insects attract attention.
(b) The man stopped his car soon after he had set out from a country village to drive to London because he heard a peculiar noise.
(c) On turning his head, the man saw something that looked like a big, dark cloud.

2   *VOCABULARY*
terrible : frightful.
especially : in particular.
avoid : escape.
discovery : being found.
sympathize : feel sorry for.
unfortunate : unlucky.
immediately : at once.

3   *PRECIS*

Points	Connections
	Connections
[1] Drove away quickly.	*In order to*
[2] Arrived London.	*and after some time*
[3] Parked car – hotel – drink.	*Parking*
[4] Customer told him : bees – car.	*When*
[5] Telephoned police.	
[6] Sent bee-keeper.	
[7] Found queen bee near wheels.	*who*
[8] Took her and bees home – box.	
[9] Motorist drove away.	*and*

The Hidden Passenger

In order to escape the bees, the motorist drove away quickly *and after some time* arrived in London. *Parking* his car outside a hotel, he went in to have a drink. *When* a customer told him that his car was covered with bees, the motorist telephoned the police. They sent a bee-keeper *who* soon found the queen bee near the wheels. He took the queen and her followers home in a box *and* the motorist then drove away in peace.

80 Words.

61

This year I decided to do something to regain my reputation as a kindly uncle. My nephew, Tony, had never forgiven me for the dictionary I had bought him as a birthday present last year. His parents had no reason to be grateful to me either, because
5 the year before, I had presented their dear son with a pot of paste and some funny pictures. Instead of sticking them into a book, Tony had naturally covered every wall in the house with them. This year, therefore, I decided to let him choose for himself.
10 We went into a big toy shop but Tony was highly critical of everything he saw. In vain did I show him toy after toy; he was not to be tempted. Then I saw his eyes light up: he had discovered something he really did approve of: a large tin drum. I was quite pleased too – until I thought what
15 Tony's mother would say when she saw it. Nobody would get any sleep for weeks! I led Tony away quickly, saying that the drum was too expensive. If that was how I felt, Tony replied jokingly, then I could buy him the big model railway in the shop window. Now that was *really* expensive, so I quickly
20 changed the subject.
Tony asked for permission to go off on his own and I made the most of my opportunity to sit down and rest my aching feet. Fifteen minutes passed but there was still no sign of Tony. I began to get worried and got up to look for him. I asked
25 a young lady if she had seen a little boy in a grey suit. She looked about her helplessly and pointed out that there were so many little boys in grey suits. I was just beginning to despair, when I saw a strange figure dressed in peculiar purple clothes. The figure was wearing a false beard and had a cave-man's axe
30 in one hand, and a space gun in the other. It was, of course, Tony who informed me at once that he was the first cave-man to fly into space.

1 *COMPREHENSION*

Give short answers to these questions in your own words as far as possible. Use one complete sentence for each answer.

(a) Why had Tony never forgiven his uncle?

(b) What had Tony done with the funny pictures his uncle had given him?

(c) Why did Tony's uncle decide not to buy the tin drum?

2 *VOCABULARY*

Give another word or phrase to replace the following words as they are used in the passage: regain (1.1); reputation (1.1); parents (1.4); grateful (1.4); funny (1.6); expensive (1.17).

3 *PRECIS*

In not more than 80 words give an account of the writer's experiences in the toy shop from the moment Tony went off on his own. Use your own words as far as possible. Do not include anything that is not in the last paragraph.

Answer these questions in note form to get your points:

[1] Why did the writer sit down after Tony went away?
[2] Did Tony return quickly or not?
[3] Did the writer look for him or not?
[4] What did the writer do when he could not find him?
[5] Could the lady help him to find Tony?
[6] Did the writer see a strange figure or not?
[7] How was the strange figure dressed?
[8] What did he have in each hand?
[9] Who was it?
[10] How did Tony describe himself?

4 *ESSAY*

Write a composition in about 200 words on *one* of the following:

(a) Suppose that the writer had not been able to find his nephew so easily. Describe what he did.

(b) Imagine that the writer bought the tin drum that Tony wanted. Describe what happened after they returned home.

62

Percy's mysterious disappearance upset everybody a great deal. Percy is a performer in a night-club and just before he was due to appear on the stage, it was discovered that he was not in his usual place. There was certainly good cause for
5 worry because Percy is a dangerous snake and he is over six feet long.

The search for Percy lasted several days and a great number of people joined in. As Percy could not possibly have gone out into the streets, he must still be hiding somewhere in
10 the club. The searchers found that some of the boards in Percy's room had rotted and there was a gap in the floor. It seemed likely that Percy had slipped under the floor and then crept behind a wall where there was a nice warm central heating unit.

15 The manager of the club suggested that Percy might have found some mice behind the wall and eaten them. Since then he had probably curled round the warm pipes and gone to sleep. As a snake that has had a satisfying meal can sleep for several days continuously, a determined effort had to be made
20 to get him out. The hot water was therefore turned off immediately and the temperature in the room fell to a few degrees above zero. But Percy, who has the reputation of being a lazy creature, made no attempt to come out. The manager then tried something else. He placed a dish full of
25 tasty delicacies near the broken floor-boards. Again Percy failed to appear. With the hot water turned off, it was decided that Percy must be freezing by now, so an electric fire was put into his room to encourage him to come in and warm himself. To help him make up his mind even more quickly, cold
30 air was blown under the floor-boards. Even these measures did not succeed, so there was only one thing left to do. The next morning, the whole wall was carefully knocked down brick by brick so as not to frighten Percy with too much noise. The hot water pipes were gradually laid bare, but, to their
35 astonishment, the searchers found no sign of Percy anywhere.

1 *COMPREHENSION*
Give short answers to these questions in your own words as far as possible. Use one complete sentence for each answer.

(a) Why was everybody worried when Percy disappeared?

(b) How long did the search for Percy last?

(c) Why did the searchers believe that Percy had hidden behind the wall?

2 *VOCABULARY*
Give another word or phrase to replace the following words or phrases as they are used in the passage: a great deal (1.1); discovered (1.3); certainly (1.4); cause (1.4); joined in (1.8); rotted (1.11); gap (1.11).

3 *PRECIS*
In not more than 80 words describe what the searchers did to find Percy. Use your own words as far as possible. Do not include anything that is not in the last paragraph.

Answer these questions in note form to get your points:

[1] Was the room warm or cold after the hot water was turned off?

[2] Did Percy appear or not?

[3] What was placed near the broken floor-boards?

[4] What was put into his room when Percy still remained hidden?

[5] Where was cold air blown?

[6] Did these measures succeed or not?

[7] What did the searchers do next morning?

[8] Why were they surprised when they laid the hot water pipes bare?

4 *ESSAY*
Write a composition in about 200 words on *one* of the following:

(a) Describe how the search for Percy continued and how he was found at last.

(b) Suppose that Percy was hiding in the club itself. Describe the scene that evening when he suddenly appeared and frightened the customers.

63

The four famous singers were due to arrive at any moment
and a large crowd of young people had gathered at the airport
to welcome them. The police found it very difficult to keep
the crowd under control after the plane came in and the singers
5　appeared. They smiled and waved gaily at everybody. Dressed
in striped pink shirts and light blue trousers, with their
hair cut short and their musical instruments over their
shoulders, the four young men looked remarkably alike.

In spite of the large number of police present, it was clear
10　that the singers would not be able to go to their waiting car
easily, for the news had got round that they had composed
a new song which would be heard when they performed in
the town that evening. They were now greeted with cries of
'Sing us a song! Sing us a song!'

15　Even the police looked pleased when the singers unstrapped
their musical instruments and prepared to sing a song as
the price of getting out of the airport. The crowd grew quiet
and listened attentively to the first performance of the new
song. As soon as it was over, there was a great burst of
20　applause and then everyone started stamping and shouting.
Several young women fainted and were quickly carried away
by policemen. Greedy for more, the crowd demanded a repeat
performance. Once again, the young men yielded, but when
the crowd requested yet another song, the singers cheerfully
25　but firmly refused. Now, closely surrounded by police, they
put away their musical instruments and went towards their
car which was some way off. The crowd pushed forward, but
policemen, locked arm in arm, prevented anyone from getting
through. It took the singers a long time to reach their car.
30　After a while, however, they were able to get in and were just
about to drive away when a young woman, who had somehow
managed to get past the police, jumped on to the roof of the
car. She shouted loudly as the police dragged her away and
the car at last moved slowly through the cheering crowd.

1   *COMPREHENSION*
Give short answers to these questions in your own words as far as possible. Use one complete sentence for each answer.
(a) Why had a large crowd gathered at the airport?
(b) Why did the singers look alike?
(c) What would be heard that evening when the singers performed in the town?

2   *VOCABULARY*
Give another word or phrase to replace the following words and phrases as they are used in the passage: famous (1.1); due to (1.1); gathered (1.2); under control (1.4); looked (1.8); alike (1.8); had got round (1.11).

3   *PRECIS*
In not more than 80 words describe what happened at the airport from the moment the musicians were asked to give a repeat performance to when they drove away. Use your own words as far as possible. Do not include anything that is not in the last paragraph.

Answer these questions in note form to get your points:

[1] Were the musicians asked to give a repeat performance or not?
[2] Did they agree to do so?
[3] Did they agree to play for a third time, or did they refuse?
[4] What did they do with their musical instruments?
[5] Where did they go?
[6] How did the police prevent the crowd from getting through to the musicians?
[7] What did a young woman do when they were just going to drive away?
[8] What did the police do then?
[9] Did the car move off or not?

4   *ESSAY*
Write a composition in about 200 words on *one* of the following:

(a) Imagine that the crowd managed to push past the police. Describe the scene that took place.
(b) Describe the performance given by the musicians later that evening in the town.

64

There was great public interest when a big hole mysteriously appeared in the middle of a field. Army mechanics and engineers were called in to explain how it had got there. They offered various explanations but were not at all sure how the
5 hole had been caused. It was thought that a large shell which must have lain buried under the ground for many years had suddenly exploded, but it was not possible to prove this.

A 'simple', but highly improbable, explanation was offered by a man who claims to be especially well-informed about
10 'flying saucers'–the strange objects which are round in shape and are said to visit the earth occasionally from outer space. The man's explanation may have been nonsense, but at least it was imaginative. At any rate, it was far more interesting than the one given by the army.

15 After examining the ground carefully, the man claimed to have seen special marks on the soil quite near the hole. These, he said, could only have been caused by a flying saucer. Moreover, the leaves on some bushes nearby had turned yellow because of a strange hot gas which had come from the saucer
20 just before it landed. Even a small tree some way off appeared to have been burnt slightly. A small piece of metal found in the hole itself provided further proof that a strange object had been there. According to the man, it was quite clear that people from another world had been circling the earth trying
25 to pick up information, when something had gone wrong. Because of this they had been forced to land in a field so that the damage could be repaired. The hole had been caused when the saucer struck the earth, while the strange marks nearby were made when it took off again. This, said the man,
30 was the simplest explanation of how the hole had appeared. Judging from the interest the public took in the matter, there must be quite a few people who secretly believe or hope that this 'simple' explanation is the true one.

1 *COMPREHENSION*

Give short answers to these questions in your own words as far as possible. Use one complete sentence for each answer.

(a) Why were army engineers and mechanics called in?
(b) How did they think the hole had been caused?
(c) What are 'flying saucers'?

2 *VOCABULARY*

Give another word or phrase to replace the following words and phrases as they are used in the passage: offered (1.4); various (1.4); exploded (1.7); highly (1.8); improbable (1.8) at any rate (1.13).

3 *PRECIS*

How did the man 'prove' that a flying saucer had visited the earth? *Do not write more than 80 words.* Use your own words as far as possible. Do not include anything that is not in the last paragraph.

Answer these questions in note form to get your points:

[1] What did the man see near the hole?]
[2] Why had the leaves on some bushes nearby turned yellow?]
[3] What had happened to a tree?]
[4] What did the man find in the hole?]
[5] What had happened when the flying saucer was going round the earth?]
[6] Why did it have to land?]
[7] How had the hole been made?]
[8] How had the strange marks been caused?]

4 *ESSAY*

Write a composition in about 200 words on *one* of the following:

(a) Suppose that the man's explanation was the true one. Describe what had happened when the flying saucer landed.
(b) Write an essay explaining how the hole had been caused. Your explanation should be different from those given in the passage.

65

Whenever I go to Westgate, I stay at the Grand Hotel. In spite of its name, it is not very grand, but it is cheap, clean, and comfortable. What is more, I know the manager well, so I never have to go to the trouble of reserving a room. The fact
5 that I always get the same room never fails to surprise me. It is situated at the far end of the building and overlooks a beautiful bay.

On my last visit, the manager told me that I could have my usual room, but he added apologetically that I might find it
10 a little noisy. So great was the demand for rooms, he told me, that the management had decided to build a new wing. I did not mind this at all. It amused me to think that the dear old Grand Hotel was making a determined effort to live up to its name.

15 During the first day I hardly noticed the noise at all. The room was a little dusty, but that was to be expected. The following afternoon, I borrowed a book from the hotel library and went upstairs to read. I had no sooner sat down than I heard someone hammering loudly at the wall. At first I paid
20 no attention, but after a while I began to feel very uncomfortable. My clothes were slowly being covered with fine white powder. Soon there was so much dust in the room that I began to cough. The hammering was now louder than ever and bits of plaster were coming away from the walls. It looked as though
25 the whole building was going to fall! I went downstairs immediately to complain to the manager. We both returned to the room but everything was very quiet. As we stood there looking at each other, I felt rather ashamed of myself for having dragged him all this way up the stairs for nothing. All
30 of a sudden, the hammering began again and a large brick landed on the floor. Looking up, we saw that a sharp metal tool had forced its way through the wall, making a very large hole right above my bed!

1   *COMPREHENSION*

Give short answers to these questions in your own words as far as possible. Use one complete sentence for each answer.

(a) Why does the writer never have to go to the trouble of reserving a room at the Grand Hotel?

(b) Where was the writer's room situated?

(c) Why did the manager think that the writer would find the room a little noisy?

2   *VOCABULARY*

Give another word or phrase to replace the following words or phrases as they are used in the passage: grand (1.2); cheap (1.2); surprise (1.5); situated (1.6); it amused me (1.12); effort (1.13); name (1.14).

3   *PRECIS*

In not more than 80 words describe what happened in the hotel room from the moment the writer went upstairs to read. Use your own words as far as possible. Do not include anything that is not in the last paragraph.

Answer these questions in note form to get your points:

[1] Where did the writer go after he had borrowed a book?
[2] What did he hear after sitting down?
[3] What were his clothes covered with?
[4] Did he begin to cough or not?
[5] What was coming away from the walls?
[6] Why did the writer go downstairs?
[7] Was there any noise when they returned?
[8] What fell on the floor when the hammering began?
[9] What made a hole in the wall?

4   *ESSAY*

Write a composition in about 200 words on *one* of the following:

(a) Imagine you were in the writer's position. Write a continuation to the passage above.

(b) Describe a visit to the hotel the following year just after the new wing had been completed.

66

Cheques have largely replaced money as a means of exchange, for they are widely accepted everywhere. Though this is very convenient for both buyer and seller, it should not be forgotten that cheques are not real money: they are quite valueless in
5 themselves. A shop-keeper always runs a certain risk when he accepts a cheque and he is quite within his rights if, on occasion, he refuses to do so.

People do not always know this and are quite shocked if their good faith is called in question. An old and very wealthy
10 friend of mine told me he had an extremely unpleasant experience. He went to a famous jewellery shop which carries a large stock of precious stone and asked to be shown some pearl necklaces. After examining several trays, he decided to buy a particularly fine string of pearls and asked if he could pay by
15 cheque. The assistant said that this was quite in order, but the moment my friend signed his name, he was invited into the manager's office.

The manager was very polite, but he explained that someone with exactly the same name had presented them with a worth-
20 less cheque not long ago. My friend got very angry when he heard this and said he would buy a necklace somewhere else. When he got up to go, the manager told him that the police would arrive at any moment and he had better stay unless he wanted to get into serious trouble. Sure enough, the police
25 arrived soon afterwards. They apologized to my friend for the inconvenience, but explained that a person who had used the same name as his was responsible for a number of recent robberies. Then the police asked my friend to copy out a note which had been used by the thief in a number of shops. The
30 note read: 'I have a gun in my pocket. Ask no questions and give me all the money in the drawer.' Fortunately, my friend's handwriting was quite unlike the thief's. He was not only allowed to go without further delay, but to take the string of pearls with him.

1   *COMPREHENSION*

Give short answers to these questions in your own words as far as possible. Use one complete sentence for each answer.

(a) Why does a shop-keeper always run a certain risk when he accepts a cheque?

(b) What did the man decide to buy?

(c) When was the man invited into the manager's office?

2   *VOCABULARY*

Give another word or phrase to replace the following words or phrases as they are used in the passage: largely (1.1); convenient (1.3); valueless (1.4); on occasion (1.6-7); wealthy (1.9); extremely (1.10); in order (1.15).

3   *PRECIS*

In not more than 80 words describe the man's experiences in the jewellery shop after he was invited into the manager's office. Use your own words as far as possible. Do not include anything that is not in the last paragraph.

Answer these questions in note form to get your points:

[1] What did the man learn from the manager? ⎤
[2] Did he get angry or not?   ⎟
[3] Why could he not leave the shop?   ⎦
[4] What did the police explain to the man?   ⎤
[5] What did they ask him to do?   ⎦
[6] Was his handwriting like the thief's or not? ⎤
[7] What was the man allowed to do after that?   ⎦

4   *ESSAY*

Write a composition in about 200 words on *one* of the following:

(a) Describe how the real thief was caught in the same shop.

(b) Imagine that the man who bought the necklace *was* the real thief. Describe how he was caught.

67

Homer, the great blind poet of ancient Greece, wrote a long account of the Trojan war in the *Iliad*. People had long been interested in finding the city of Troy, but the only man who took Homer's description seriously was Heinrich Schliemann.
5 Using Homer as his guide, Schliemann discovered what was almost certainly the ancient city of Troy. Though he had made it his aim to find Troy as a young man, Schliemann was only able to realize his ambitions after he had become a successful merchant.
10 Schliemann at once realized that the spot in Asia Minor generally believed to be Troy did not match Homer's detailed description. According to Homer, a palace of sixty rooms had been built on a hill and the Greeks had marched between their ships and the city several times a day. The hill on which
15 Troy was supposed to have been built was not only very small, but was a great distance from the sea as well.
Much nearer the sea, Schliemann came across a bigger hill. Homer had written that Achilles and Hector had run round the walls of Troy three times while fighting each other. Having
20 calculated that this would have been possible, Schliemann decided to dig. It was not long before he discovered the remains of a city—not Troy, but a much later one called New Ilium. When his workmen dug deeper, Schliemann was most surprised to find that there were no less than nine cities built on
25 top of each other. But which of these was Troy? Homer again provided Schliemann with two important facts: the city had been built of stone and had been burnt to the ground by the conquering Greeks. Schliemann believed that the second city must have been Troy, for he found the ruins of a palace and
30 a large gate blackened by fire. Yet the most astonishing discovery was still to come. After noticing something shining in the soil, Schliemann got so excited that he dug with his bare hands. He unearthed the beautifully preserved treasure of King Priam: gold, silver, and jewellery, thus completing one
35 of the most important historical discoveries ever made.

1 *COMPREHENSION*

Give short answers to these questions in your own words as far as possible. Use one complete sentence for each answer.

(a) What use did Schliemann make of Homer's *Iliad*?
(b) When was Schliemann able to realize his ambitions?
(c) Why would it not have been possible for the Greeks to march to the sea several times a day from the small hill on which Troy was supposed to have been built?

2 *VOCABULARY*

Give another word or phrase to replace the following words as they are used in the passage: account (1.2); ancient (1.6); aim (1.7); merchant (1.9); realized (1.10); did not match (1.11); supposed (1.15).

3 *PRECIS*

In not more than 80 words describe how Schliemann discovered the city of Troy. Use your own words as far as possible. Do not include anything that is not in the last paragraph.

Answer these questions in note form to get your points:

[1] What did Schliemann see near the sea?
[2] Did he calculate that it would have been possible to run round it or not?
[3] What was the name of the city he found after digging?
[4] How many cities did he find in all?
[5] What did the discovery of a palace and a large gate blackened by fire tell him?
[6] What did he notice in the soil?
[7] Did he dig with a spade, or with his bare hands?
[8] What did he find?

4 *ESSAY*

Write a composition in about 200 words on *one* of the following:

(a) Imagine that Schliemann told his own story. Write a first person account.
(b) Describe any important discovery of the same type that has been made in your own country.

68

The first man to jump out of an aeroplane when travelling at a speed greater than sound was Arthur Ray Hawkins, one of the most outstanding United States Navy pilots. Jumps of this sort had long been regarded as impossible.

5 During an air show over Mississippi in 1954, Hawkins was flying an entirely new type of plane. At 40,000 feet, the nose of the plane dipped sharply. No matter how hard he tried, Hawkins could not pull it out of the dive and it gathered such speed that it was soon travelling faster than sound. Strapped

10 in his seat, and hanging upside-down, the pilot could not reach the button which would destroy the top of the plane. Near him however, there was another button which was to be used only in times of very great danger. Hawkins pressed it. There was an explosion and his seat – which shielded him to

15 some extent – burst through the glass shell above his head. While still half conscious, Hawkins tried to pull the ribbon which would open his parachute. It was fortunate that he failed in his attempt, for at such a rate of speed, the parachute would have been torn to pieces. As he sped towards the

20 earth, he realized that the breathing-tube which supplied him with air had also been torn away. Rapidly losing consciousness because of the lack of air, he knew that he had to open the parachute – otherwise he might not get another chance to do so. At about 29,000 feet, the parachute opened and Hawkins

25 pulled a handle which freed him from the pilot seat. While swinging through the air in slow motion, he began to tremble with cold and everything went grey: he was not getting enough air! Just then, he remembered a rule for breathing at great heights. He took short, sharp breaths and so forced air into

30 the bloodstream. This kept him alive until, at 10,000 feet, he could breathe without difficulty. Soon afterwards, he landed safely in a field of cotton. His plane crashed into a wood nearby, but luckily no one was hurt.

1   *COMPREHENSION*

Give short answers to these questions in your own words as far as possible. Use one complete sentence for each answer.

(a) Where did the air show take place?
(b) Why did the aeroplane travel faster than sound?
(c) Why was Hawkins unable to reach the button which would destroy the top of the aeroplane?

2   *VOCABULARY*

Give another word or phrase to replace the following words or phrases as they are used in the passage: at a speed greater than (1.2); outstanding (1.3); regarded (1.4); entirely (1.6); type (1.6); shielded (1.14); to some extent (11.14-15).

3   *PRECIS*

In not more than 80 words describe Hawkins' experiences after he went flying into space. Use your own words as far as possible. Do not include anything that is not in the last paragraph.

Answer these questions in note form to get your points:

[1] Why was it lucky that Hawkins failed to open his parachute after he jumped out of the plane?
[2] Why did he open the parachute at 29,000 feet?
[3] Did he begin to lose consciousness after he freed himself from the pilot seat or not?
[4] How did he breathe at this height?
[5] When could he breathe easily?
[6] Where did he land?

4   *ESSAY*

Write a composition in about 200 words on *one* of the following:

(a) Imagine you had to jump in a parachute from an aeroplane. Describe your experiences.
(b) The first flight into space.

69

Some people seem to have been born with an unfailing sense of direction. Even when lost in a forest, they find their way home as surely as a dog picks up the scent of a hunted man. The secret is probably that they never *feel* lost. Others, like
5 myself, can even manage to get lost in a department store.
While in the army there was nothing I disliked so much as the map-reading course, for the simple reason that I *always* feel lost–even with a map in my hand. For weeks I had lain awake at night thinking of the practical test I would have to
10 face at the end of the course. At last, the evil day arrived. It was to be my responsibility to lead a small band of soldiers back to camp from the middle of nowhere. We were driven out in a closed lorry and left in a ploughed field with instructions to get back to camp as quickly as possible.
15 Well knowing my abilities, the soldiers smiled as they saw me looking at the map and they made all sorts of helpful suggestions. I folded the map up, put it in my pocket, and said that we would head east. After walking through cornfields for over an hour we came to a wide stream. I again looked
20 at the map. It seemed to be covered with masses of thin blue lines, but which particular line was *this* stream? In despair, we sat down in the cool shade and I felt like throwing the map into the water. About fifteen minutes later, a boat passed and I asked the boatman if he could give us a lift to
25 the nearest village. I pretended that we had been out for a walk and somehow got lost. The boatman invited us on board and I felt very foolish when he told me that he had helped hundreds of soldiers to pass their map-reading test! Not long afterwards, we got off the boat and, following the boatman's
30 instructions, took a bus into the village. When we got back to camp, the Commanding Officer congratulated me on having led the men back so quickly!

1   *COMPREHENSION*

Give short answers to these questions in your own words as far as possible. Use one complete sentence for each answer.

(a) Why, in the writer's opinion, do some people have a good sense of direction?
(b) What would the writer have to do at the end of the map-reading course ?
(c) How did the writer and the soldiers reach the ploughed field?

2   *VOCABULARY*

Give another word or phrase to replace the following words as they are used in the passage: unfailing (1.1); forest (1.2); scent (1.3); disliked (1.6); test (1.9); evil (1.10); band (1.11).

3   *PRECIS*

In not more than 80 words describe how the soldiers got back to camp from the moment the writer put the map in his pocket. Use your own words as far as possible. Do not include anything that is not in the last paragraph.

Answer these questions in note form to get your points:

[1] Did the writer put the map away or not?
[2] In which direction did he lead the party?
[3] Did they cross corn-fields or not?
[4] Where did they arrive?
[5] Could the writer find the stream on the map?
[6] Did they sit down in the shade or not?
[7] What passed then?
[8] What did the writer ask the boatman?
[9] Were they invited on board or not?
[10] What did the boatman tell them to do when they got off ?
[11] Did they return to camp quickly from the village or not?

4   *ESSAY*

Write a composition in about 200 words on *one* of the following:

(a) Describe how the writer was given a second test during which he failed completely to get back to camp.
(b) Imagine that the Commanding Officer found out that a boatman had been helping soldiers in their map-reading test. Describe what he did.

70

Hunting was originally a means of providing food, but it has now become a sport. Though in some parts of the world there are still people who hunt wild animals to provide themselves with food, in England, hunting is as much a social activity
5 as anything else.

A great many years ago, fishermen in Japan used birds to catch fish. This art of fishing is said to be at least a thousand years old and is mentioned in Japanese Nohukai plays. Today, however, fishing in this way has simply become a sport, for the
10 fishermen are not seriously interested in catching fish.

On summer nights the fishing boats set out on rivers in various parts of the country. At the front of each boat there is an iron basket in which a wood fire is kept burning. As the graceful curved boats float past carried along by the current,
15 these fires, dotted here and there, make bright patterns on the water. Steering down the river, the fishermen beat the sides of the boat to encourage the birds, and people out for an evening's entertainment either sit or lie on the floor of the boats drinking beer and sometimes even cooking a meal for
20 themselves over the flames of the fire. This method of fishing demands great skill, for the fisherman has to handle three or four birds in one hand. A long piece of string is tied round the neck of each bird and the fisherman must take care to keep the birds separate from each other. Every so often, the birds
25 are set free and they fly close to the water is search of fish. The moment a bird catches a fish in its beak, it is pulled back on to the boat. The string is held tightly round the bird's throat to prevent it from swallowing the fish it has caught. When there do not seem to be many fish in the river, the fisher-
30 men can sometimes be seen secretly throwing dead fish into the water for the birds to catch. No one really objects to this practice, as it is all part of this unusual sport.

1 *COMPREHENSION*

Give short answers to these questions in your own words as far as possible. Use one complete sentence for each answer.

(a) What was the original purpose of hunting?
(b) Why are the Japanese fishermen mentioned in this passage not seriously interested in catching fish?
(c) In which season of the year do the fishing boats set out?

2 *VOCABULARY*

Give another word or phrase to replace the following words as they are used in the passage: originally (1.1); means (1.1); provide (1.3); mentioned (1.8); various (1.11); country (1.12); beat (1.16).

3 *PRECIS*

In not more than 80 words, give an account of this art of fishing from line 16 ('Steering down the river . . .') to the end. Use your own words as far as possible. Do not include anything that is not in the last paragraph.

Answer these questions in note form to get your points:

[1] What do the fishermen do to encourage the birds?   ]
[2] How many birds does the fisherman have in one hand?   ⎤
[3] What is tied round the neck of each bird?   ⎥
[4] What must the fisherman take care to do?   ⎦
[5] What does the fisherman do after the bird catches a fish?   ⎤
[6] Why is the string held tightly?   ⎥
[7] What do fishermen sometimes throw into the water?.   ⎤
[8] Why do they have to do this?   ⎦

4 *ESSAY*

Write a composition in about 200 words on *one* of the following:

(a) Imagine a fisherman describing this sport to you. Write a first person account.
(b) The day I went fishing.

To the teacher

Comprehension, Vocabulary, and Essay questions are of the same type as those that appear in passages 61-70. At this stage, however, the student will be expected to write a summary entirely on his own. He should be trained to follow the instructions carefully. His précis work will fall into three distinct parts: (a) making a list of points, (b) writing a rough draft, (c) writing a fair copy.

To the student

Comprehension, Vocabulary and Essay questions will be no different from those that appear in the first half of the Chapter. But you will now be expected to write a precis entirely on your own. Follow the instructions carefully.

How to Work
[1] Read the instructions which will tell you where your précis will begin and end, and exactly what you will have to do.
[2] Read again the part of the passage that you will have to summarize.
[3] Write a list of points *in note form*. Do not include unnecessary facts.
[4] Connect your points to write a *Rough Draft* of the précis in your own words. Refer to the passage only when you want to make sure of some point. *Do not* count the number of words until you have finished your Rough Draft.
[5] In the Rough Draft it is likely that you will go well over the word limit. Correct your Draft carefully, bringing the number of words down to the set limit. You may write fewer than 80 words, but you must *never* write more.
[6] Write a Fair Copy of your précis stating the exact number of words you have used at the end.
[7] Give your précis a title.
[8] Neatly cross out your points and your Rough Draft.

Carefully work through the example given below and note how each question has been answered.

Example

The total number of cars in Britain now exceeds 11,000,000. Traffic goes on increasing all the time and the roads of most big cities are almost permanently blocked by a slow moving procession of metal cages. Complicated systems of one-way
5 streets and the universal use of traffic lights have not provided a real solution of the problem. As far as the motorist is concerned, driving in crowded towns is far from being a pleasure.

Some time ago, a friend of mine who works in a part of the
10 city I do not know very well, invited me to call on him. It took me hours to get there and I drove round and round looking for a convenient spot to park my car. At last I found a small space in a backstreet. As I was already three quarters of an hour late, I parked my car quickly and hurried off on foot.
15 Making my way rapidly along the street, I could not help reflecting that, nowadays, it is much easier to walk than to drive.

At noon, just as I was leaving my friend's office, it suddenly struck me that I had no idea where I had parked my car. I
20 could hardly go up to a policeman and tell him that I had lost a small green car somewhere! I would simply have to look for it myself. Walking down street after street, I examined each car closely and was greatly relieved to see a small green car just behind an old cart. But how disappointed I was to
25 discover that though the car was exactly like my own, it belonged to someone else! Feeling quite tired now, I gave up the search and went off for lunch. Some time later, I left the restaurant and walked idly down the street. Turning the corner, I nearly jumped for joy: my car was right in front of
30 me—and there was no mistaking it this time. I could not help smiling as I drew near. Pasted on the wind-screen was a little ticket which informed me that the car had been visited by a policeman in my absence. To add to it all, I was now guilty of a traffic offence!

1   *COMPREHENSION*
    Give short answers to these questions in your own words as far as possible. Use one complete sentence for each answer.

(a) Why are the roads of most big cities almost permanently blocked?
(b) What did the writer do after he arrived near his friend's office?
(c) Why did the writer park his car in a hurry?

2   *VOCABULARY*
    Give another word or phrase to replace the following words and phrases as they are used in the passage: exceeds (1.1); increasing (1.2); permanently (1.3); universal (1.5); pleasure (1.8); a convenient spot (1.12); reflecting (1.16).

3   *PRECIS*
    In not more than 80 words describe the writer's experiences after he left his friend's office. Use your own words as far as possible. Do not include anything that is not in the last paragraph.

4   *ESSAY*
    Write a composition in about 250 words on *one* of the following:

(a) Imagine that the writer's search proved to be even more difficult. Write an account of it.
(b) Suppose that you were driving the car and could not find anywhere to park at all. Describe what you did.

POSSIBLE ANSWERS
1   *COMPREHENSION*
(a) The roads of most big cities are almost permanently blocked because the number of cars is getting bigger and bigger.
(b) After he arrived near his friend's office, the writer tried to find a place to park his car.
(c) The writer parked his car in a hurry because he was late for his appointment.

2   *VOCABULARY*
    exceeds: is more than.
    increasing: getting bigger and bigger.
    permanently: continuously.
    universal: general.
    pleasure: joy.
    a convenient spot: a suitable place.
    reflecting: thinking.

3   *PRECIS*

Points

[1]   Could not remember.
[2]   Walked down street after street.
[3]   Examined each car.
[4]   Saw small green one.
[5]   Same – but someone else's.
[6]   Gave up search.
[7]   Went for lunch.
[8]   Left restaurant.
[9]   Walked down street.
[10]   Turned corner – found car.
[11]   Saw ticket – windscreen – police.

Rough Draft

Because the writer could not remember where he had left his car, he walked down street after street looking carefully at all the parked cars. At last, he saw a small green one which was just the same as his but which belonged to someone else. He now gave up the search and went to a restaurant for lunch. He left the restaurant some time later and walked down the street. When he turned the corner, he suddenly found his car. As he went closer, he noticed that there was a police ticket on the wind-screen.

97 Words

Fair Copy

The Lost Car.

Unable to remember where he had parked, the writer went down street after street looking carefully at each car. At last, he saw a small green one which looked like his own but belonged to some-one else. He now gave up the search and went for lunch. On leaving the restaurant some time later, he walked down the street and suddenly found his car just round the corner. As he drew near, he noticed a police ticket on the wind-screen.

80 Words

71

The great midnight feasts we used to have are one of my happiest memories of boarding school. Our housemaster, Mr Beamish, had an evil reputation and these feasts had to be organized with considerable skill. Each feast was something
5 of an adventure and afforded countless opportunities for deeds of daring.
I remember one occasion particularly well. The new term had begun and, of course, a feast had been arranged. There was great excitement during the day and our masters must have
10 wondered what it was all about. There were remarkably few complaints at tea-time and some boys did not eat anything at all. Later that evening, punctual as ever, Mr Beamish turned the lights off at ten o'clock. We could be punished for talking after 'lights out', but it was difficult to keep quiet. At about
15 eleven o'clock, Jones and Pringle at last overcame their fears. They crept up to the window and drew the curtains slightly to see if Mr Beamish's light had been turned off. It was still on and we waited impatiently for ages, sorry to have given our housemaster so much marking to do.
20 When his light went out at last, we all jumped out of bed. Evans produced a wax candle which he set in the middle of the floor. In no time the place was covered with cakes, fruit, nuts, and gallons of soft drink. We even persuaded Knobbly Jones to give up his mother's fruitcake – not an easy thing to
25 do! Even then we found that he had reserved a very large piece for himself, wrapped up in one of the sheets. It must have been about one o'clock when some of us were falling asleep on the floor and only a few hardy ones were still eating that Knobbly dropped his mother's cake tin. There was a loud
30 crash and, gathering up the remains of the feast which we slipped under the bed-clothes, we quickly retired to bed. It was a good thing we acted so rapidly, for a few minutes later the door opened and Mr Beamish appeared – only to find twenty little boys sleeping gently!

1 *COMPREHENSION*

Give short answers to these questions in your own words as far as possible. Use one complete sentence for each answer.

(a) Why was it necessary to organize midnight feasts with considerable skill?
(b) What were the boys not allowed to do after 'lights out'?
(c) Why did the boys have to wait a long time before beginning the feast?

2 *VOCABULARY*

Give another word or phrase to replace the following words as they are used in the passage: considerable (1.4); afforded (1.5); countless (1.5); deeds (1.6); masters (1.9); punctual (1.12); drew (1.16).

3 *PRECIS*

In not more than 80 words describe what the boys did after Mr Beamish's light was turned off. Use your own words as far as possible. Do not include anything that is not in the last paragraph.

4 *ESSAY*

Write a composition in about 250 words on *one* of the following:

(a) Imagine that Mr Beamish interrupted the boys during the feast. Describe what happened.
(b) Write an imaginary account of the character of Mr Beamish showing how he gained his 'evil reputation'.

72

Animals are seldom officially employed, so it was strange to learn that a cat was formally appointed as a member of staff in a government department. The cat, called Peta, is classed as an industrial civil servant and earns a salary of £13 per
5 year. She got the job because the cat employed before her had died and because she has a fine reputation. As a member of the Board of Agriculture said, 'though still young, she has already caught several mice on the farm where she was born.'
10 Peta was flown into London, travelling as excess baggage. When she arrived at the Home Office, she received very special treatment. Even a film actress might have envied her. A government minister took time off to welcome her and it was found necessary to limit the number of reporters and
15 photographers so as not to frighten her.
Sitting on a large leather-topped desk, Peta looked over her shoulders at photographers. She was not in the least disturbed by flashing cameras and the questions asked by reporters. Quite at ease, she looked up at them with her big
20 yellow eyes as if to ask what all the excitement was about. Just then, a reporter took a grey toy mouse from his pocket, wound it up, and placed it on the desk. The mouse began to 'run' in circles, until Peta gave it a sharp blow with her paw and sent it flying off the desk. Everybody expected her to
25 run after it, but she remained quite still. It was clear that she could not be deceived by a clock-work mouse. Suddenly she jumped off the table and walked round the room. Reporters felt sure she must be looking for a mouse hole. Instead, however, she began to stretch herself in a ray of sun-light coming
30 in through the window. It was decided that she must be tired after her journey and she was taken downstairs to her basket. But Peta soon discovered that she had a great deal of work to do, for with no cat around, the mice had been playing happily for a long time.

1 *COMPREHENSION*
   Give short answers to these questions in your own words as far as possible. Use one complete sentence for each answer.

(a) Why was it strange to learn that a cat was formally appointed as a member of staff in a government department?
(b) What qualifications did Peta have for the job?
(c) Why might a film actress have envied Peta when she arrived in London?

2 *VOCABULARY*
   Give another word or phrase to replace the following words as they are used in the passage: seldom (1.1); employed (1.1); salary (1.4); excess (1.10); envied (1.12); limit (1.14); frighten (1.15).

3 *PRECIS*
   In not more than 80 words describe what Peta did during her meeting with reporters and photographers. Use your own words as far as possible. Do not include anything that is not in the last paragraph.

4 *ESSAY*
   Write a composition in about 250 words on *one* of the following:

(a) Describe a day in Peta's life at the Home Office.
(b) Suppose Peta could tell her own story. How would she describe her first day in London?

It is not necessary to go to the Himalayas to do some climbing. It is not even necessary to have a mountain: an old university building can provide quite as many excitements. Indeed, it can often provide more, since climbing buildings is absolutely
5 forbidden and for this reason can only be done at night.

One night, two students decided to fix a flag on 'Luther's Pinnacle', the highest point of a rival college. This was regarded as a particularly dangerous operation, for the building had not been climbed since 1911; moreover it was extremely
10 unsafe. But both students possessed those rare qualities common to great climbers: skill and daring.

Just after midnight, the students climbed up a rusty pipe which brought them on to the roof of the main building. Round about, tall towers rose up above their heads, and
15 looking down on them all, was the forbidding sight of 'Luther's Pinnacle'. The students next climbed up an arch which had been put up fairly recently and was therefore not too difficult. Then, balancing themselves on the top, they both jumped across a great gap and were now beneath the Pinnacle itself.
20 The delicate stonework had been worn smooth by wind and rain over the centuries. Ugly stone heads with twisted smiles on their faces looked down on them scornfully. One of the students seized one of the heads and part of it came away in his hands. It was an awkward moment, but they were deter-
25 mined not to give up now. The climbers tested each stone to make sure it was safe before stepping on it, but in spite of the care they took, loose stones kept slipping away when they leant on them. The wind screamed around them and there were times when they thought that the whole Pinnacle would crash
30 down. At last they reached the very top and pushed a flag into the hollow mouth of a devilish head on the highest point. As they looked down on the dark mass of buildings below, they knew very well what questions would be asked in the morning.

1 *COMPREHENSION*
Give short answers to these questions in your own words as far as possible. Use one sentence for each answer.

(a) Why can climbing old university buildings often provide more excitement than climbing mountains?

(b) Give two reasons why it was considered to be particularly dangerous to climb 'Luther's Pinnacle'.

(c) What qualities should a good climber have?

2 *VOCABULARY*
Give another word or phrase to replace the following words and phrases as they are used in the passage: quite (1.3); absolutely (1.4); forbidden (1.5); for this reason (1.5); fix (1.6); operation (1.8); possessed (1.10).

3 *PRECIS*
In not more than 80 words describe what the students did during the climb. Use your own words as far as possible. Do not include anything that is not in the last paragraph.

4 *ESSAY*
Write a composition in about 250 words on *one* of the following:

(a) Describe how the students climbed down again from the top of the Pinnacle.

(b) Describe what happened the next morning at the college when the flag was discovered.

74

According to the advertisement, the cottage was two minutes'
walk from the bus stop, in an excellent state of repair, and
built high up on the chalk cliffs, with a glorious view of the
sea. A house agent had also recommended the place to me,
5 informing me that the rent was moderate and that the landlady
was 'a very pleasant person'.
I calculated I had been walking for fifteen minutes before I
recognized the cottage. It was at the very edge of a bare
cliff. The view of the sea was indeed wonderful, but I was
10 surprised to find that the fence round the cottage was badly
damaged, and even more surprised to discover that the garden
was neglected and full of weeds. When I rang the bell, a
woman appeared at a window and roughly asked me what I
wanted. Her sour expression turned into a smile of welcome
15 the moment I explained, and I was led into a dark unfriendly
hall.
Inside, the house smelled damp and I immediately felt that
my trip had been a waste of time. However, I followed the
woman into a room at the back of the house. As soon as she
20 opened the door, we were greeted by a cold wind that blew
fiercely through a broken window. The plaster was cracked
and the walls badly stained with ink and finger marks. Suddenly, I saw another door and asked where it led to. As I
got nearer I was astonished to find that someone had scratched
25 his name on the paint-work. The woman did not seem eager
to open the door, but I insisted so much that at last she
unlocked it. What I saw did not encourage me to stay a
moment longer. The door led to a small yard in which there
was the biggest collection of rubbish I have ever seen: old
30 tyres, newspapers, bottles, tins, decaying shoes and clothes,
and an ancient, rusty, iron pump. I hurriedly thanked the
woman for the trouble she had taken and left the 'delightful'
cottage as quickly as I could.

1   *COMPREHENSION*
    Give short answers to these questions in your own words as
    far as possible. Use one complete sentence for each answer.

(a) Why did the house agent recommend this house to the writer?
(b) Why was the writer surprised when he got near the cottage?
(c) What happened when the writer rang the bell?

2   *VOCABULARY*
    Give another word or phrase to replace the following words
    and phrases as they are used in the passage: an excellent state
    of repair (1.2); glorious (1.3); moderate (1.5); calculated (1.7);
    edge (1.8); indeed (1.9); neglected (1.12).

3   *PRECIS*
    In not more than 80 words describe what the writer saw and did
    after he entered the house. Use your own words as far as
    possible. Do not include anything that is not in the last
    paragraph.

4   *ESSAY*
    Write a composition in about 250 words on *one* of the following:

(a) Suppose the writer rented the room he saw. Describe his life
    in the cottage.
(b) Imagine that the woman wrote a letter to her sister (an equally
    unpleasant person) describing the writer's visit.

75

Many tourists must have dreamed of owning a small house in a foreign country—perhaps on a stretch of lonely coast— to which they could return year after year to enjoy the sun and the sea. Others, with even bigger ideas and a lot more
5 money to spend, think of buying hotels. In any case, it is absolutely essential to know a great deal about the value of property—otherwise the buyer may be at the mercy of dishonest agents.

Some tourists, however, are so foolish that they really deserve
10 to be cheated by agents. We would consider a person mad if he walked into a museum and asked to 'buy' a great work of art. Though no one has told us, we all know that certain things can *never* be sold, no matter how much money is offered. Yet, nearly every year since 1944, a buyer has been found for the
15 Colosseum in Rome. The first one was a soldier who parted with his money for what was described as 'a rather broken down and heavily damaged building . . . in a good position.'

The people of Rome eagerly look forward to each year's 'sale'. They were amused to learn that, as usual, a tourist
20 recently expressed the desire to buy the historic building. Two agents told him that the building was in need of repair, but the buyer could expect a high return for his capital. They took him to the Colosseum itself and pointed out that the top floor would make a wonderful international restaurant.
25 It was in an ideal position and offered a fine view of the city of Rome. Besides, for some strange reason, so many people wished to visit the building that the buyer would make a considerable profit on entrance tickets. In the agents' opinion, it was well worth spending money on a building like this.
30 They asked the buyer for a mere 200,000 lire as a deposit and told him they would complete arrangements that evening at a certain hotel. The tourist was sure that he had bought a bargain and later went to the hotel to meet the agents. But, of course, they never came.

1 *COMPREHENSION*
   Give short answers to these questions in your own words as
   far as possible. Use one complete sentence for each answer.

(a) Why should tourists thinking of buying a house abroad know
    a great deal about the value of property?
(b) Why would we consider a person mad if he walked into a
    museum and asked to buy a work of art?
(c) Who was the first person to 'buy' the Colosseum?

2 *VOCABULARY*
   Give another word or phrase to replace the following words as
   they are used in the passage: owning (1.1); foreign (1.2);
   essential (1.6); property (1.7); otherwise (1.7); cheated (1.10);
   position (1.17).

3 *PRECIS*
   In not more than 80 words describe what happened when a
   tourist expressed the wish to 'buy' the Colosseum. Use your
   own words as far as possible. Do not include anything that is
   not in the last paragraph.

4 *ESSAY*
   Write a composition in about 250 words on *one* of the following:

(a) Imagine that the tourist was under the impression that he had
    really bought the Colosseum and was free to do as he pleased.
    Describe what happened.
(b) Suppose that the agents went to the hotel that evening to
    meet the tourist again. Continue the passage above.

76

The writers of murder stories go to a great deal of trouble to keep us guessing right up to the end. In actual fact, people often behave more strangely in real life than they do in stories.

5 The following advertisement once appeared in a local newspaper: 'An opportunity to earn £250 in a few minutes. A man . . . willing to take chances wanted for an out-of-the-ordinary job which can be performed only once.' A reader found this offer very generous and applied to the advertiser,

10 but being a bit suspicious, he gave a false name. Soon afterwards, he received a reply. Enclosed in the envelope was a typed note instructing him to ring a certain number if he was still interested. He did so and learnt on the telephone that the advertiser wanted him 'to get rid of somebody' and would

15 discuss it more fully with him next day. But the man told the police and from then on acted under their instructions.

The police saw the two men meet and watched them as they drove away together. In the car the advertiser came to the point at once: he told the man he wanted him to shoot his

20 wife. The reason he gave was that he was suffering from an incurable disease and wanted to live in a warmer country, but his wife objected to this. Giving the man some money, the advertiser told him to buy a gun and warned him to be careful of the dog which, though it would not bite, might

25 attract attention. He also gave him a photograph of his wife so that he would be able to recognize her. After that, the advertiser suggested that the man should 'do the job' next morning. Meanwhile, he would prepare his wife by telling her that a young man was going to call. After the murder, they

30 would meet again outside a railway station and the money would be paid as arranged. The second meeting never took place, for the advertiser was arrested shortly afterwards and charged with attempting to persuade someone to murder his wife.

1   *COMPREHENSION*

Give short answers to these questions in your own words as far as possible. Use one complete sentence for each answer.

(a) What do the writers of murder stories try to do?
(b) What sort of person did the advertisement in the newspaper ask for?
(c) Why did the reader give a false name when he answered the advertisement?

2   *VOCABULARY*

Give another word or phrase to replace the following words as they are used in the passage: behave (1.3); opportunity (1.6); being (1.10); a bit (1.10); false (1.10); reply (1.11); discuss (1.15).

3   *PRECIS*

In not more than 80 words write an account of what the advertiser told the man after they drove away together. Use your own words as far as possible. Do not include anything that is not in the passage.

4   *ESSAY*

Write a composition in about 250 words on *one* of the following:

(a) Imagine that the man referred to in the passage had not gone to the police and that he agreed to do what the advertiser wanted. Describe what happened.
(b) Describe how the advertiser was arrested by the police. Write an imaginary account of what he told them.

I lose so many things that I could swear they just get up and walk. Perhaps I have never admitted it—even to myself, but I am extremely jealous of people who are so orderly that they never lose anything. Most of my friends always seem to have
5 a place for everything and everything is in its place. I hate comparing myself with them. They have special cupboards for tools, hooks to hang things on and drawers to put things in. It is quite impossible for me to compete.

Some things have a terrible habit of making themselves
10 scarce the moment I need them. Pencils and ball-point pens are never anywhere near the telephone when it rings, no matter how much care I take. Screw-drivers and tin-openers always manage to wander out into the garden and, as a result, screws remain loose· and tins remain unopened. Boxes of matches
15 slide under the radio, and needles disappear every time I want to sew a button on a shirt.

The situation was getting so much out of control that I decided to organize myself. I had a large cupboard put into the kitchen. On the shelves I neatly arranged a number of
20 boxes and tins the contents of which I clearly printed in ink on the outside. I had one box for pins, another for nails, and a special place for screw-drivers. There was a new address book in one corner so that I could make a note of telephone numbers and addresses. Before this I had always written addresses
25 on bits of paper—which I promptly lost. Soon everything was tidily arranged in its place, from pairs of scissors to cakes of soap and spare lamps. Having made such a sincere attempt to prevent things from running away, I felt very proud of myself. But it was not long before the matches
30 disappeared and the hammer decided to hide itself in the waste-paper basket. I soon got my revenge, however. I had a lock fitted to the cupboard and thus made sure than nothing could escape. This was an admirable solution—until I lost the key to the cupboard!

1   *COMPREHENSION*

Give short answers to these questions in your own words as far as possible. Use one complete sentence for each answer.

(a) Why does the writer hate comparing himself with others?
(b) When does the writer need pencils and ball-point pens?
(c) Why do screws remain loose and tins unopened?

2   *VOCABULARY*

Give another word or phrase to replace the following words and phrases as they are used in the passage: jealous (1.3); orderly (1.3); hate (1.5); making themselves scarce (11.9-10); the moment (1.10); remain 1.14); slide (1.15).

3   *PRECIS*

In not more than 80 words describe what steps the writer took to prevent things from disappearing. Use your own words as far as possible. Do not include anything that is not in the last paragraph.

4   *ESSAY*

Write a composition in about 250 words on *one* of the following:

(a) Describe how the writer found the key to the cupboard and how, in a short time, he managed to lose everything in it. Write in the first person.
(b) Describe your own experiences in not being able to find things you need.

78

These days we are so accustomed to telegraph messages that it is hard for us to imagine the excitement that was felt in the nineteenth century when the first cables were laid.

Cable laying proved to be immensely difficult. The cable which in the autumn of 1850 carried the first telegraph messages between England and France had a very short life. The day after, a fisherman 'caught' the cable by mistake. Thinking that the copper wire at the centre of the thick cable was gold, he cut a piece off to show his friends. However, a new cable was put down and soon news could travel quickly across Europe. But there was still no way of sending messages between Europe and America.

When the Atlantic Telegraph Company was formed in 1856, a serious attempt was made to 'join' Europe to America with no less than 2300 miles of cable. As no single ship could carry such a weight, the job was shared by two sailing vessels, the *Agamemnon* and the *Niagara*. The intention was, that after setting out in opposite directions, they should meet in the middle of the Atlantic Ocean where the two cables would be connected together. But the ships had hardly covered 300 miles when the cable broke. In 1858, a second attempt was made. This time, greatly hindered by storms, the ships were again unsuccessful. There was great rejoicing a few months later, when after the combined efforts of both ships, Britain and America were at last connected by cable and the Queen of England was able to speak to the President of the United States. This cable, however, only lasted eleven weeks. Further attempts were postponed until 1864 when Brunel's steamship, the *Great Eastern,* set forth. This powerful ship did the whole job by itself, but again messages could not travel freely because the cable developed a fault. While it was being mended, it broke and 1300 miles of it lay on the ocean floor. But two years later the *Great Eastern* completed a highly successful journey and since then it has become possible to send messages to all parts of the world.

1 *COMPREHENSION*
   Give short answers to these questions in your own words as
   far as possible. Use one complete sentence for each answer.

(a) When was the first telegraph cable laid?
(b) Why did the fisherman think that the cable he had 'caught'
    was valuable?
(c) How many miles of cable were needed to join Europe to
    America?

2 *VOCABULARY*
   Give another word or phrase to replace the following words
   and phrases as they are used in the passage: accustomed (1.1);
   hard (1.2); laid (1.3); immensely (1.4); by mistake (1.7); at the
   centre (1.8); way (1.11).

3 *PRECIS*
   In not more than 80 words describe how a cable was laid
   between Britain and America, from line 20 ('But the ships . . .')
   to the end. Use your own words as far as possible. Do not
   include anything that is not in the last paragraph.

4 *ESSAY*
   Write a composition in about 250 words on *one* of the following:

(a) Write an imaginary account of the third successful journey of
    the sailing vessels *Agamemnon* and *Niagara*.
(b) Imagine the fisherman 'catching' the cable. Write a first person
    account of what he did.

79

In the twentieth century numerous new nations have been formed. Though their peoples often enjoy full political liberty, there exist at the same time a great many strange practices. Native populations may be free to vote and to elect whom they please to govern them, but popular prejudices, unusual and harmful customs take a long time to die out. However, now that people are better educated, they need not suffer in silence, for they are able to express their views. With the spread of civilization, improved living conditions, the cheapness of radio sets, books and newspapers, most people are fairly well-informed. In this way many unpleasant customs disappear rapidly.

There was a good example of this recently in a newly formed republic when a girl of fourteen refused to marry a sixty year old man who had 'bought' her for £40. Her father had agreed to the marriage when the girl was only four years old and had 'sold' her to a man who already had at least six wives. Just before the marriage ceremony, the girl ran away and wrote to the president of the republic. In her letter she pointed out that although her country was independent, its people were still not truly free. Some human beings were like slaves, she said, and women could be bought and sold like cattle. She asked the president if he felt that this was right. This letter caused the president a great deal of concern and he immediately changed the cruel law which permitted women to be bought and sold.

The girl had won a considerable victory but she still had a big problem. She had to find £40 to repay the man who might have become her husband. There seemed to be no way of raising so much money. Fortunately, however, the girl's story was broadcast on a radio programme in Europe and nearly £2000 poured in from listeners. The buyer got his money back and the girl was free to marry anyone she chose. She had won true freedom for herself and for others like her.

1   *COMPREHENSION*
Give short answers to these questions in your own words as far as possible. Use one complete sentence for each answer.

(a) What sometimes prevents people in newly formed nations from enjoying true freedom?
(b) What has been the effect of the spread of education and improved living conditions?
(c) To whom was the girl 'sold'?

2   *VOCABULARY*
Give another word or phrase to replace the following words and phrases as they are used in the passage: nations (1.1); liberty (1.2); elect (1.4); please (1.5); to die out (1.6); views (1.8); improved (1.9).

3   *PRECIS*
In not more than 80 words describe what the girl did to win her freedom and explain how money was collected to pay back the man who had 'bought' her. Use your own words as far as possible. Do not include anything that is not in the passage.

4   *ESSAY*
Write a composition of about 250 words on *one* of the following:

(a) Write an account of the broadcast which brought in money to help the girl.
(b) Suppose you were in the girl's position. Write a letter to the president of the republic.

80

The fact that everybody enjoys a good mystery explains why magicians are such popular entertainers. We all know that a magician does not really depend on 'magic' to perform his tricks, but on his ability to act at great speed. However, this
5 does not prevent us from enjoying watching a magician produce rabbits from a hat, swallow countless eggs, or saw his wife in two.

Probably the greatest magician of all time was Harry Houdini who died in 1926. His real name was Ehrich Weiss, but he
10 adopted the name 'Houdini' after reading a book which influenced him greatly. This had been written by a famous magician called Robert-Houdin. Houdini mastered the art of escaping. He could free himself from the tightest knots or the most complicated locks in seconds. Although no one
15 really knows how he did this, there is no doubt that he had made a close study of every type of lock ever invented. He would carry a small steel needle-like tool strapped to his leg and he used this in place of a key.

Houdini once asked the Chicago police to lock him in prison.
20 They bound him in chains and locked him up, but he freed himself in an instant. The police accused him of having used a tool and locked him up again. This time he wore no clothes and there were chains round his neck, waist, wrists, and legs; but he again escaped in a few minutes. Houdini had
25 probably hidden his 'needle' in a wax-like substance and dropped it on the floor in the passage. As he went past, he stepped on it so that it stuck to the bottom of his foot. His most famous escape, however, was altogether astonishing. He was heavily chained up and enclosed in an empty wooden
30 chest the lid of which was nailed down. The chest was dropped into the sea in New York harbour. In one minute Houdini had swum to the surface. When the chest was brought up, it was opened and the chains were found inside.

1 *COMPREHENSION*

Give short answers to these questions in your own words as far as possible. Use one complete sentence for each answer.

(a) Why are magicians such popular entertainers?
(b) Why did Weiss adopt the name of 'Houdini'?
(c) What did Houdini use to open locks?

2 *VOCABULARY*

Give another word or phrase to replace the following words and phrases as they are used in the passage: popular (1.2); prevent (1.5); watching (1.5); saw (1.6); influenced (11.10-11); escaping (1.13); in seconds (1.14).

3 *PRECIS*

In not more than 80 words give an account of Houdini's experiences as described in the last paragraph. Use your own words as far as possible.

4 *ESSAY*

Write a composition in about 250 words on *one* of the following:

(a) Describe what Houdini did in the box after it was dropped into the sea.
(b) Describe a performance given by a magician.